# Perpetual War

# for Perpetual Peace

NUMBER FIVE

Foreign Relations and the Presidency

H. W. Brands, General Editor

# Perpetual

# War for

# Perpetual

# Peace

ROBERT A. DIVINE

*Texas A&M University Press*
*College Station*

Copyright © 2000 by Robert A. Divine
Manufactured in the United States of America
All rights reserved
First edition

The paper used in this book meets the minimum requirements
of the American National Standard for Permanence
of Paper for Printed Library Materials, z39.48-1984.
Binding materials have been chosen for durability.

∞

*In association with*
*The Center for Presidential Studies*
*George Bush School of Government and Public Service*


Library of Congress Cataloging-in-Publication Data

Divine, Robert A.
  Perpetual war for perpetual peace / Robert A. Divine.—
1st ed.
      p.   cm.—(Foreign relations and the presidency ; no. 5)
  Includes bibliographical references (p.) and index.
  ISBN 0-89096-953-1 (alk. paper);  1-58544-105-8 (pbk.)
  1. United States—History, Military—20th century.
  2. United States—Foreign relations—20th century—
Philosophy.   3. National characteristics, American.
  I. Title.   II. Series
  E745.D58    2000
  327.73—dc21                              00-020198

FOR DARLENE

# Contents

# Acknowledgments

In the spring of 1998, Prof. H. W. Brands of Texas A&M University asked me if I would give a series of lectures on his campus in the fall as part of the Program in Foreign Relations and the Presidency offered under the auspices of the Center for Presidential Studies. I quickly accepted this gracious request from a former student and decided that America's involvement in the wars of the twentieth century would be an appropriate topic. The reflections that follow, with the exception of the epilogue on Kosovo that was written later, originated as lectures at the George Bush School of Government and Public Service, Texas A&M University, in early November, 1998.

In preparing these lectures, I relied heavily on more than forty years of teaching diplomatic history at the University of Texas. In a sense, they reflect a distillation of the ideas and concepts that I offered to undergraduates who took my course in twentieth-century American diplomatic history. I am deeply indebted to my fellow diplomatic historians whose work and ideas helped shape my own view of the history of American foreign policy. The notes in each essay refer only to the sources for quotations; a full listing of the many scholars on whose work I have relied would be far too long to include.

Finally, I wish to express my gratitude to Bill Brands, who made this venture possible. He proved to be a generous host during my visit to his campus, and he encouraged me to transform the lectures into this book. I view him not only as a former student but also as a colleague and a friend.

# Perpetual War

# for Perpetual Peace

# Introduction

Americans like to think of themselves as a peace-loving people and the United States as a peaceful nation. Yet just a glance at our history reveals America's long involvement in war from colonial times to the present—from our role in British imperial struggles of the eighteenth century down to the recent Cold War with the Soviet Union.

There has not been a single American generation that did not take part in a war. We capped our colonial experience with the French and Indian War, a nine-year struggle to oust the French from North America. We gained our independence from England only after fighting for seven years in the Revolutionary War. In the nineteenth century, the nation was involved in a bloody conflict every few decades—beginning with the frustrating War of 1812, which ended in a stalemate; the 1846 war with Mexico, which fulfilled America's manifest destiny; the bloody Civil War, which featured American fighting American; and ending with the 1898 war with Spain, a one-sided contest that marked America's emergence as a world power.

In the twentieth century, war has played an equally important role in our history. In 1917 Woodrow Wilson led America into the Great War that had begun in Europe in 1914 in a self-proclaimed attempt to make the world safe for democracy. Its failure to achieve that idealistic goal was made evident by the outbreak of World War II just over twenty years later, culminating in America's entry after the 1941 Japanese attack on Pearl Harbor. Even though the United States emerged from that conflict as by far the most powerful nation on earth, instead of enjoying an era of peace, it quickly plunged into the Cold War. While the fear of nuclear devastation made engaging in hostilities with the Soviet Union unthinkable, America kept getting involved in limited wars designed to halt communist expansion, most notably in Korea, which like the War of 1812 ended in stalemate, and Vietnam, the first war we lost. Finally, the end of the Cold War by 1990 was quickly followed by America's swift if ambiguous victory over Iraq in the Persian Gulf War.

The record speaks for itself: war has been an integral part of our history. Much as we profess the desire for a tranquil and peaceful world, we have resorted to arms again and again, engaging in what Harry Elmer Barnes aptly described as "perpetual war for perpetual peace."[1]

I admit that there is some risk in borrowing the title of a book by a controversial scholar who was a leading revisionist on both world wars—a historian who believed that the United States engaged in "interminable wars, disguised as noble gestures for peace." Barnes's curious combination of broad learning and polemical writing led one observer to label him "Half Savanarola and half Diderot." It is interesting to note that Barnes himself credits the phrase "perpetual war for perpetual peace" to another controversial yet distinguished historian: Charles A. Beard. According to Barnes, Beard used the phrase in their last conversation in 1947 to sum up twentieth-century American foreign policy. Both Beard and Barnes damaged their reputations by accusing Franklin D. Roosevelt of leading America into World War II by deceitful and underhanded means. While I disagree with this charge, I still find that their analysis of American involvement in foreign wars has merit. In refuting isolationism, orthodox historians have too often embraced, in Barnes's words, "militarism, the crusading spirit, and war hysteria."[2] Now that the Cold War is over and we have begun a new millennium, it is time to take a more critical look at the record of American involvement in the wars of the twentieth century.

In these pages, I explore the historical record in an effort to determine if there is indeed a distinctive American style of war. Is there something in our democratic creed that leads us into hostilities so often? Does the American sense of mission demand that we take up arms on a regular basis in an effort to transform the world into our own image? Or are there baser motivations—the quest for territory, the search for markets, the simple lust for power—that drive us into these conflicts?

In an effort to find an answer, I focus on America's involvement in the wars of the twentieth century. The first chapter examines the process of going to war, seeking a distinctive pattern in how America became involved in hostilities. The second deals with the way America fights its wars—with how the nation views the use of force to achieve political ends. The final chapter concentrates on how America brings wars to an end, which, I believe, may shed the most light of all on our national character.

# CHAPTER ONE

# Entering Wars

As a democratic nation, the United States has always sought justification for the use of force. Americans like to think of themselves as a peaceful people who take up arms only when provoked. George Kennan gave the most striking analogy to illustrate this national trait in his 1950 Walgreen lectures. He likened the United States to a prehistoric beast, "with a body as long as this room and a brain the size of a pin," oozing blissfully in the slime, impervious to its surroundings. But every once in a while there would be an outside stimulus that would finally provoke the monster, causing it to rise from its sloth, destroy whatever was tormenting it, along with much of the environment, and then sink back blissfully into the primeval mud.[1]

This trait led in the nineteenth century to a pattern of drawing a line in the sand, daring an enemy to move beyond it, before the United States would take up arms. The best example is the way Pres. James K. Polk handled the crisis with Mexico in 1846. When Mexico broke off diplomatic relations after America annexed Texas, Polk responded by ordering Brig. Gen. Zachary Taylor to move his army from Corpus Christi across a disputed zone of south Texas to take up positions at present-day Brownsville on the northern bank of the Rio Grande. Polk clearly wanted to provoke Mexico into firing the first shot, but at first he was frustrated by Mexican forbearance. Finally, in early May, 1846, he told his cabinet he planned to ask Congress for a declaration of war. When he retired to the White House to write the war message, trying desperately to find enough grievances to justify such a step, one of the great coincidences in history occurred. A dispatch rider arrived at the White House bearing news that a week earlier Mexican forces had crossed the Rio Grande and had engaged Taylor's army in battle. A jubilant Polk cast aside his first draft and quickly wrote a new message to Congress, ending with this famous peroration: "As war exists, and not withstanding all our efforts to avoid it, exists by the Act of Mexico herself, we are called upon by every consideration of duty and patriotism to vindicate with decision the honor, the rights and the interests of our country."[2]

This pattern of prolonging a crisis and waiting for the other side to make the first overt move became standard operating procedure. In 1861, as the Southern states began to secede from the Union, Pres. Abraham Lincoln resisted making increased demands for an armed response. Instead, he waited for the South to make the first move. His patience was finally rewarded when Confederate forces fired on Fort Sumter in Charleston, South Carolina. Lincoln quickly rallied the nation, calling on the Northern states to supply seventy-five thousand men to suppress this armed insurrection. A wave of patriotic fervor swept over the previously divided North. "It seems as if we were never alive till now," wrote one New Yorker, "never had a country till now."[3] By letting the South fire the first shot, Lincoln was able to lead a united North into a bloody civil war.

The war with Spain three decades later also came about by waiting on events. William McKinley had tried hard to seek a peaceful resolution to the crisis in Cuba, where rebels used guerrilla tactics in an effort to oust the Spanish. Led by William Randolph Hearst and Joseph Pulitzer, the "Yellow Press" screamed for war, feeding an alarmed nation exaggerated reports of Spanish atrocities against the Cuban people. Yet it took the dramatic sinking of the battleship *Maine* in Havana harbor in early February, 1898, to create the public demand for hostilities that compelled McKinley to insist that the Spanish give Cuba its freedom. When Spain refused to give way, the cry "Remember the *Maine;* To Hell with Spain!" echoed across the country and led to war by mid-April.[4]

Thus the pattern for American involvement in foreign wars was set by the time the United States became a rising world power at the outset of the twentieth century. As a peaceful, democratic country, it would never commit an act of aggression or initiate hostilities; instead it would wait until its opponents made the first move. But America frequently engaged in provocative behavior, drawing a line and daring an adversary to cross it. Such a pattern enabled Americans to cherish their belief in the country's devotion to peace while engaging regularly in just wars—conflicts begun by the enemy and fought in the name of self-defense.

## A War to End All Wars

America's first twentieth-century war, known by contemporaries as the Great War, revealed a slight alteration in the prevailing pattern. Once again the United States drew a line, and when the enemy crossed it, war became nearly certain. But Pres. Woodrow Wilson attempted to put his own personal stamp on the decision for war by trying to impose the idealistic goal of fighting a war to end all wars rather than simply defending America's national interests. His failure to achieve that utopian war aim led to profound disillusionment.

When the conflict began in August, 1914, most Americans were glad that the nation's traditional policy of isolation protected the United States from automatic involvement. America was not part of the entangling alliances that had divided Europe into two armed camps—the Allies (England, France, and czarist Russia) and the Central Powers (Germany and the Austro-Hungarian Empire). When the fighting on the western front settled down into a bloody stalemate, the American people tended to sympathize with the Allies and to reap great profit from trade with Britain and France due to their control of the sea. By 1915 the American economy was tied irrevocably to the Allied cause. Trade with Germany evaporated as a result of the British blockade, while exports to England and France increased dramatically, financed in large part by loans from American bankers like J. P. Morgan.

American sympathy for the Allies was not solely the product of economic ties. A common language and heritage bound America closely to England, the former mother country. Strategic considerations played a role as well. The United States had nothing to fear from an Allied victory, but a German triumph might well lead the victor to challenge America's dominance in the Western Hemisphere. In the nineteenth century, Britain had maintained the balance of power in Europe; Germany threatened to upset that equilibrium, with consequences that might prove dangerous. But whatever the long-run danger, there was no immediate threat that required American involvement in the brutal European struggle.

It was the German U-boat menace to American trade that compelled Woodrow Wilson to draw the line in 1915. When the German government first announced it would engage in unrestricted submarine warfare early that year, Wilson invoked the principle of freedom of the seas in announcing that he would demand "strict accountability" for any German violation of American rights. When a U-boat sank the British liner *Lusitania* in May, killing nearly twelve hundred people, including 128 Americans, Wilson held Germany responsible for what he considered a cowardly and dishonorable act. Although he had originally warned only against attacks on American ships, he broadened his policy to include the right of Americans to travel on belligerents' ships. The issue, at bottom, was not protecting passengers, but rather Wilson's determination to defend American trade with England and France.

Germany backed down in 1915, accepting blame for the

*Lusitania* incident and promising not to attack passenger liners again. But as the stalemate continued on the western front, German military leaders advised Kaiser Wilhelm that they could not win the war without choking off the Allies's Atlantic supply line. On January 31, 1917, Germany informed the United States that it intended to resume unrestricted submarine warfare, threatening to sink any American vessel that tried to reach England or France. Hoping that this was only a bluff, Wilson responded by severing diplomatic relations. When Germany began sinking American ships in the Atlantic in March, Wilson knew he had no choice but to declare war. Once again, America had drawn a line and the enemy had crossed it.

This time, however, Wilson sought a higher justification for American participation in the European slaughter. When he addressed a special session of Congress on April 2, 1917, he said that German actions in the Atlantic amounted to war against the United States. But in asking for a formal declaration of war, he went on to stress more noble and idealistic concerns than mere defense of America's maritime interests. He elevated the conflict into an American effort to share its democratic values with all mankind. "We are glad," he proclaimed, "... to fight thus for the ultimate peace of the world and for the liberation of its peoples, the German peoples included: for the rights of nations great and small and the privilege of men everywhere to choose their way of life and of obedience. The world must be made safe for democracy."[5]

Wilson went on to disavow any selfish motives. America sought no indemnities, he promised, no colonies, no reparations, no material advantage. Instead, warning of the sacrifices that lay ahead, he called upon the American people to fight "for democracy, for the right of those who submit to authority to have a voice in their own governments, for the rights and liberties of small nations, for a universal dominion of right by such a concert of free peoples as shall bring peace and safety to all nations and make the world at last free."[6]

They were noble sentiments, nobly expressed. But in promising to fight a war to end all wars, Wilson was making a commitment he could not keep. Aware of the need to justify repudiating the age-old policy of isolation from European wars, Wilson appealed to America's oldest and highest ideals: it was a land of virtue and freedom fulfilling its historic mission to share its blessings with the entire world. His rhetoric succeeded in unifying the nation and insuring victory, but at the same time he sowed the seeds of disillusion and despair. The gap between the nobility of his dream and the postwar reality would prove too great; when the war failed to achieve his high goals, the American people felt betrayed. No one expressed the high toll of the war on the American psyche better than George Creel, who headed the wartime agency charged with spreading Wilson's message to the world. Writing in 1920, Creel lamented: "On the day of the armistice, America stood on the hilltops of glory, proud in her strength, invincible in her ideals, acclaimed and loved by a world free of an ancient fear at last: today we writhe in a pit of our own digging, despising ourselves and despised by the betrayed peoples of earth. Instead of unity a vast disintegration, instead of enthusiasm an intolerable irritation, instead of fixed purpose a strange and bewildering indecision."[7]

## Making the World Safe for the United States

Renowned diplomatic historian Samuel Flagg Bemis claimed that Woodrow Wilson went to war in 1917 on the right side for the wrong reason. Instead of stressing the national economic and security interests that would be jeopardized by German victory, Wilson unwisely transformed the conflict into a great moral crusade. When war broke out in Europe again in 1939, Franklin D. Roosevelt was careful not to repeat the mistakes of his Democratic predecessor. Playing down the moral issue (and thus, ironically, the real evil of Adolf Hitler's Nazi regime), FDR instead focused on the threat Germany posed to America's national interests. In contrast to Wilson, Roosevelt fought to make the world safe for the United States.

The outbreak of war in 1939 came just as the country was beginning to shake the grip of isolationism. As war loomed in the mid-1930s, the American people, still reacting against World War I, vowed not to be fooled a second time. From 1935 to 1937, Congress passed three neutrality laws designed to prevent the one-sided trade with the Allies that many believed had led to war in 1917. The key feature was a mandatory embargo on the export of arms to any belligerent, whether an aggressor or the victim of aggression. But as Hitler took over Austria and then, after the folly of British and French appeasement at Munich, Czechoslovakia as well, many Americans began to see Nazi Germany as a genuine threat to American security.

After the German invasion of Poland on September 1, 1939, finally led England and France to declare war, FDR persuaded Congress to repeal the arms embargo, replacing it with a cash-and-carry policy designed to provide American resources to the Allies at minimal risk of U.S. involvement. The new policy of aiding the Allies short of war got a huge boost after the German blitz in the spring of 1940. As the powerful German war machine drove the British off the continent at Dunkirk and forced France to surrender in just six weeks, Americans began to feel threatened. If Britain went under, the Western Hemisphere might become Hitler's next target. As the American people revealed their sympathy for a beleaguered Britain, listening to Edward R. Murrow's harrowing broadcasts during the aerial blitz of London, Roosevelt was able to end any pretense of neutrality and began a policy of all-out aid to those resisting German aggression. In a speech at Charlottesville, Virginia, in June, 1940, he warned his countrymen of the peril they faced and the risk of trying to ignore the new realities:

Some indeed still hold to the now somewhat obvious delusion that we of the United States can safely permit the United States to become a lone island, a lone island in a world dominated by the philosophy of force. . . . Such an island represents to me and to the overwhelming majority of Americans today a helpless nightmare, the helpless nightmare of a people without freedom; yes the nightmare of a people lodged in prison, handcuffed, hungry, and fed through the bars from day to day by the contemptuous, unpitying masters of other continents. . . . Overwhelmingly we, as a nation—and this applies to all the other American nations—are convinced that military and naval victory for the gods of force and hate would endanger the institutions of democracy in the Western world, and that equally, therefore, the whole of our sympathies lies with those nations that are giving their life blood in combat against these forces.[8]

Notice that Roosevelt did not denounce Hitler's crimes or call for a crusade against an evil regime. Instead he concentrated on the threat Nazi Germany posed to the United States.

During the next year, FDR undertook two actions that gave substance to his new policy of all-out assistance to the Allies short of war. In September, 1940, he announced the transfer of fifty American destroyers to Britain for convoy duty in exchange for air and naval bases on eight British possessions in the Atlantic. The justification was self-defense: If Britain fell, the bases, ranging from Newfoundland to Trinidad, would be vital to guard against any future German attack. The following spring, Congress enacted the Lend-Lease Act, effectively canceling the "cash" part of cash-and-carry and allowing the flow of arms and war supplies to Britain to continue without payment. In a now-famous press conference, FDR defended the idea of loaning England planes, tanks, and ships, likening it to lending a neighbor a garden hose when his house was on fire. Presumably the neighbor would return the hose when the fire was out. This in turn led Republican senator Robert Taft to object. Lending arms, said Taft, was "a good deal like lending chewing gum. You don't want it back."[9] By mid-1941, with the destroyers-for-bases deal and lend-lease, FDR had led the nation halfway into the European war and was stuck. Isolationists in Congress prevented him from going any farther, while interventionists in his cabinet urged him to end the charade and ask for a declaration of war. Roosevelt instead fell back on traditional American tactics: he would attempt to provoke Hitler into firing the first shot.

But FDR's attempts to force a clash with Germany in the North Atlantic failed because Hitler refused to cooperate. The German dictator did nothing to oppose the American occupation of Greenland and later Iceland to prevent Germany from establishing submarine bases on those islands. The U.S. Navy also began sending patrols halfway across the Atlantic to assist the British in combating German U-boats. When the destroyer *Greer* tangled with a German submarine in early September, FDR called the U-boats "the rattlesnakes of the Atlantic" and ordered the navy to use its destroyers to protect British convoys in the western half of the Atlantic.[10] Although this bold policy led to the torpedoing of two destroyers, Hitler refused to rise to the bait and instead ordered his submarine commanders not to attack American ships except in self-defense. Remembering the decisive role the United States had played in World War I, the mercurial Hitler frustrated FDR by displaying remarkable restraint.

Stymied in the Atlantic, FDR turned to the Pacific and drew the line that finally led to war. Throughout the 1930s the United States had limited itself to formal protests as Japan seized Manchuria, invaded China, and developed plans to create a Greater East Asia Co-Prosperity Sphere. From the beginning, Roosevelt viewed Germany as the greater danger and gave Hitler top priority while trying to postpone a showdown with Japan. But the global nature of the threat became apparent in September, 1940, when Germany, Japan, and Italy signed the Tripartite Pact—a defensive alliance that Hitler hoped would deter the United States by confronting FDR with the prospect of a two-ocean conflict.

Roosevelt began to firm up American policy against Japan

in 1941 as Tokyo started to move into the southern half of French Indochina, threatening all of the resource-rich area of Southeast Asia. When diplomatic initiatives failed, the president decided to use American economic power to halt Japan's advance. On July 26, 1941, the United States froze all Japanese assets, thereby terminating trade between the two countries. The real purpose of the freeze was to stop the shipment of petroleum to Japan, which was heavily dependent on oil from the United States and the Dutch East Indies, whose output was controlled by American companies. Apparently FDR intended only to get Japan's attention, planning to ease restrictions in return for Japanese concessions. But strong support for the oil embargo, both in the nation at large and within the administration, led to it becoming permanent by the end of August.

With the oil clock ticking, Japan was faced with a difficult choice. Japanese leaders could give in to American pressure and renounce their plans for expansion or they could go to war and seize the oil they needed in the Dutch East Indies. Once again, the United States had drawn a line and surrendered the initiative to its opponent. This traditional American maneuver almost proved fatal in 1941. Under the cover of last-minute negotiations, Japan launched its devastating strike at Pearl Harbor, crippling the U.S. Pacific Fleet and enabling Japanese forces to sweep across Southeast Asia and seize the Dutch East Indies.

Pearl Harbor proved to be a brilliant tactical move by Japan. However, it was a strategic disaster. The sneak attack unified a divided nation. Roosevelt termed December 7 "a date which will live in infamy" in asking Congress to declare war. There was only one dissenting vote in both houses.[11] Hitler then proved cooperative, declaring war on the United States and allowing Roosevelt to achieve his goal of complete involvement in World War II. Once fully engaged, the United States displayed the power and will to defeat Japan nearly single-handedly and to play a major role in ending Hitler's dream of a thousand-year Reich.

Once again the United States had waited on events. The need

to convince the reluctant American public to go beyond all-out aid short of war dictated such a policy. After the conflict Roosevelt's critics charged that he had taken the "back door to war." They claimed that he deliberately exposed Pearl Harbor to Japanese attack to get the nation into the European war.[12] Although there is no evidence of such a plot, it is true that Roosevelt was less than candid with the American people. When he failed to provoke Hitler into firing the first shot in the Atlantic, he pursued a policy that forced Japan to take its desperate gamble. But he could not have anticipated Hitler's irrational act in declaring war after Pearl Harbor. If the Nazi leader had continued his restrained policy, the United States would have had no choice but to fight Japan alone, giving Hitler the chance to defeat England and the Soviet Union in Europe. America's habit of waiting for its adversaries to strike the first blow had jeopardized the national interest; fortunately, Hitler's impulsive act enabled the United States to insure his ultimate demise.

## In Defense of Collective Security?

On June 25, 1950, North Korean forces crossed the 38th Parallel and invaded the Republic of Korea. Pres. Harry S. Truman responded by branding North Korea the aggressor and asking the United Nation's Security Council to call upon all UN members to join the United States in upholding the principle of collective security. By the end of June, the president had committed American troops to battle under the UN banner without asking Congress for a declaration of war. Recalling the appeasement of aggressors that had preceded World War II, Truman was convinced he had no choice. "Communism was acting in Korea just as Hitler, Mussolini, and the Japanese had acted ten, fifteen, and twenty years earlier," he wrote in his memoirs.[13]

The subsequent Korean War was America's first limited war. Formally labeled "a police action," it reflected the realities of the nuclear age. With the Soviets possessing the atomic bomb by

1950, Truman was intent on limiting the conflict to the Korean peninsula and fighting it under the authority of the United Nations. Yet in reality, the Korean War was essentially a civil war between the forces of Kim Il Sung in the north and Syngman Rhee in the south. As for the nominal role of the United Nations, the supreme commander, Gen. Douglas MacArthur, later commented: "The entire control of my command and everything I did came from our own Chiefs of Staff. . . . I had no direct connection with the United Nations whatsoever."[14]

Ostensibly, the outbreak of the Korean War fit the pattern of earlier American conflicts. America drew a line at the 38th Parallel and, when the enemy crossed it, responded vigorously. But the line was purely arbitrary, chosen in 1945 simply as a way of separating Soviet troops entering Korea from Manchuria from American forces landing in the south. When UN efforts to form a unified Korean government failed, the United States backed Rhee's regime in the south, albeit with some misgivings, while Joseph Stalin supported Kim in the north. When Kim told Stalin of his decision to use force to gain control of all Korea he gained only reluctant approval and grudging support from the Soviet premier.

The Korean War eventually sparked heated controversy within the United States over how it should be fought, a topic I will cover in the next chapter, but there was no debate over the decision to fight in 1950. The American people rallied behind Truman's call to arms, seeing the conflict as both a genuine effort to uphold the principle of collective security and a necessary attempt to halt Communist expansion. Even Truman's harshest Republican critic, Sen. Robert Taft, backed the war, criticizing the president only for not securing congressional approval for a formal declaration of war.

In retrospect, it would have been far wiser had Truman followed the normal constitutional procedures. When controversy over conduct of the war arose later, it was easy for critics to lampoon a "police action" and to ridicule the pretense that it was a United Nations effort. Unlike Wilson and Roosevelt, Truman had failed to offer a compelling rationale for war and he suffered the consequences when the conflict turned ugly.

## *Vietnam: Into the Quagmire*

If the Korean War is an exception to the general pattern for American involvement in foreign wars, then Vietnam is even more difficult to explain in terms of drawing a line and waiting for your adversary to fire first. America's involvement in Vietnam is most often likened to a quagmire. The United States gradually but inexorably moved deeper and deeper into a morass, unable to pull back and becoming further entrapped with each effort to overcome the obstacle. In essence, America entered the Vietnam conflict by incremental steps, beginning with Truman's decision to extend economic and military aid to the French in 1950 and culminating in Lyndon Johnson's massive escalation from 1965 to 1968.

President Johnson inherited an impossible commitment from his White House predecessors. Truman had made the original decision to include Vietnam within the policy of containment. His military and diplomatic advisers told him that Vietnam was the key to Southeast Asia and that if America lost this region, "we shall have suffered a major political rout the repercussions of which will be felt throughout the rest of the world."[15] Truman announced the decision to help France defeat Communist guerrillas in May, 1950; the outbreak of the Korean War a month later confirmed the American belief that Moscow was masterminding a takeover of all Asia. President Dwight D. Eisenhower extended the American commitment to defend Vietnam after the French defeat at Dien Bien Phu. The United States replaced France as the main sponsor of the Republic of Vietnam, the new regime in Saigon holding sway south of the 17th Parallel. By the time John F. Kennedy became president, the Vietcong, aided by North Vietnam, were waging an intense guerrilla war in the southern countryside. Kennedy felt bound by the pledges of his predecessors; he accelerated American economic and military assistance to Saigon and increased the number of U.S. military advisers from less than a thousand to more than seventeen thousand by 1963. More ominously, he permitted dissident generals to overthrow South Vietnamese president Ngo Dinh Diem, thereby creating a power vacuum in Saigon that only the United States could fill.

For Lyndon Johnson, Vietnam was like the dreaded Queen of Spades in "Old Maid." There were two rules to the Vietnam variation of this card game. First, the United States had to prevent the Communists from taking over all of Vietnam before the next presidential election. Second, the United States must never fight another land war in Asia. Truman, Eisenhower, and Kennedy had all played the game skillfully, each passing on the Old Maid to his successor. But time had run out on LBJ; he would either have to concede Vietnam to the Communists or commit U.S. troops to a war on the Asian mainland.[16]

Despite considerable agonizing, Johnson ended up pursuing the second alternative. He had pledged to continue Kennedy's policies at home and abroad. Moreover, he was a staunch advocate of the containment policy that had led to the Vietnam fiasco. His difficulty lay in finding an explanation that would rally the nation behind an unpopular Asian war. He maintained that Vietnam was vital for the world balance of power, but that case was weak. Ho Chi Minh was clearly not a Soviet puppet, and the growing split between China and Russia made the concept of a monolithic Communist threat almost ludicrous. Johnson kept hammering at the need to defend democracy in South Vietnam, but few could find much devotion to self-government among the corrupt and dictatorial men wielding power in Saigon. Ultimately, LBJ had to fall back on the issue of credibility: A great power like the United States had to keep its word or no ally would ever again trust it. Assistant Secretary of Defense John McNaughton summed it up best when he said that there was only one reason why America had not withdrawn from Vietnam: "to preserve our reputation as a guarantor, and thus to preserve our effectiveness in the rest of the world."[17] The irony, of course, is that America's stubborn insistence on keeping its pledge to defend South Vietnam shocked its European allies. Instead of bolstering U.S. credibility in the eyes of the world, the escalation in Vietnam appeared to America's friends as truly incredible and made them question American judgment and reliability.

In implementing his Vietnam policy, Lyndon Johnson also fell back on the tried and true national habit of appearing to respond to an enemy's aggressive acts. His first move came in the summer of 1964 when North Vietnamese torpedo boats attacked the *Maddox,* an American destroyer engaged in electronic surveillance of the North Vietnamese coastline while South Vietnamese guerrillas conducted a raid nearby. The *Maddox* beat off the attack, but the next day the *Maddox* and the *Turner Joy,* another destroyer sent to help out, reported a second North Vietnamese attack. Subsequent investigation indicated there was no second attack, but Johnson, refusing to wait for confirmation, ordered retaliatory air strikes and asked Congress to pass the Gulf of Tonkin resolution, giving him virtually a blank check to wage war against North Vietnam in the future. Johnson acted primarily to keep Barry Goldwater, his Republican opponent in the 1964 presidential race, from making Vietnam an important campaign issue. There is no evidence he had yet decided to increase American involvement in the conflict. Unfortunately, as Edward Moise points out, that was exactly the conclusion drawn by Hanoi, which responded by sending North Vietnamese combat units down the Ho Chi Minh Trail to join the Vietcong in the south. "The overall result," writes Moise, "was that by the time the United States began major escalation . . . the Communist forces with which the Americans had to deal were stronger, better prepared, and better supplied than they would have been had the Tonkin Gulf incidents never occurred."[18]

The second example of exploiting a hostile enemy move to justify the use of force came in February, 1965. After his reelection, Johnson's military advisers told him that unless the United

States began using its airpower, South Vietnam was doomed to defeat. By January, the Joint Chiefs of Staff had approved plans for both retaliatory air strikes (Operation Flaming Dart) and the sustained bombing of North Vietnam (Operation Rolling Thunder). When the Vietcong carried out an attack on a U.S. Army barracks at Pleiku on February 6, Johnson decided to strike back, authorizing Flaming Dart. Within a week, the president approved the implementation of Rolling Thunder. The bombing of targets in North Vietnam would continue, with only brief pauses, for the next three years.

McGeorge Bundy, LBJ's national security adviser, later revealed the cynical nature of American policy. When asked what would have happened if there had not been an attack on Pleiku, he replied, "Pleikus are like streetcars." In other words, it would have been easy to catch the next streetcar, that is, the next Vietcong attack, to justify the aerial assault.[19]

A month later, Johnson was forced to send in marines to protect U.S. air bases in South Vietnam, and in July, with little public fanfare, he began the massive buildup of American ground forces that totaled over a half-million troops by 1968. Yet unlike Franklin Roosevelt, who had used devious means to align the United States against Nazi Germany in 1940 and 1941, LBJ was unable to escape the growing public dissent. His deceptive use of the incidents in the Tonkin Gulf and at Pleiku resulted in a credibility gap; the American people believed that the president had deceived them. Support for the war eroded as the escalation continued and the body count grew, until finally Johnson could not appear in public without hearing derisive jeers and cries of "Hey, hey, LBJ, how many kids have you killed today?"[20] Moreover, as the U.S. military used its massive firepower to devastate the countryside, America became an international pariah, accused of destroying the very nation it claimed to be defending. Johnson had indeed become the Old Maid. Like a figure in a Greek tragedy, he watched helplessly as Vietnam destroyed his presidency.

## Ideals versus Self-Interest

The 1991 Persian Gulf War was far briefer and far more successful than the Vietnam conflict. Yet it also reveals the continuing American difficulty with justifying the use of arms. The war against Iraq was clouded by uncertainty over exactly what U.S. troops were fighting for: Was it the liberation of Kuwait or guaranteed access to Persian Gulf oil?

The way the war came about was almost a complete reversal from the American habit of drawing a line and daring an adversary to cross it. When Saddam Hussein invaded Kuwait on August 2, 1990, the Bush administration was caught off guard. Thinking the Iraqi leader was only bluffing with his troop buildup and threats against Kuwait, Pres. George Bush and his advisers had to move quickly to make sure that Saddam did not sweep into Saudi Arabia and seize the vast oil reserves in the region.

America's lack of anticipation dated back to the 1980s, when the United States backed Iraq against Iran in the long war between those two nations. Despite Iraq's close ties to the Soviet Union and Saddam's brutal regime, the Reagan administration reestablished diplomatic relations with Baghdad in 1984 and quietly gave Iraq considerable economic assistance. The United States refrained from denouncing Saddam's use of poison gas against Kurdish villages, and when two Iraqi Exocet missiles hit the USS *Stark,* nearly sinking it and taking thirty-seven lives, the United States was quick to accept Iraq's apology for the tragic "accident." After the war with Iran ended in 1988, America underwrote large-scale agricultural exports to Iraq and pursued a policy of "engagement" in an effort to offset the perceived threat of Iran to the peace and stability of the Persian Gulf area.

The American effort to curry favor with Saddam evidently led him to believe he could seize Kuwait without provoking an American response. On July 25, as he stepped up the pressure against his neighbor, Saddam met with April Glaspie, the U.S.

ambassador to Iraq. Far from drawing a line, she told the Iraqi leader that she had "direct instructions" from President Bush to seek better relations with Iraq and then repeated the State Department's position that the United States had "no opinion on the Arab-Arab conflicts, like your border disagreement with Kuwait."[21] America preferred to rely instead on other Arab countries, primarily Jordan and Egypt, to broker a peaceful settlement of Iraq's dispute with Kuwait.

After the invasion of Kuwait, the Bush administration moved quickly to defend an exposed Saudi Arabia. Within three days, the president told reporters, "This will not stand, this aggression against Kuwait." He dispatched a mission to Saudi Arabia and, when King Fahd proved amenable, announced that U.S. troops would defend the Saudi kingdom against an attack. In explaining Operation Desert Shield to the American people on August 8, Bush called for "the immediate, unconditional and complete withdrawal of all Iraqi forces from Kuwait." However, he went on to say that "the mission of our troops is wholly defensive. . . . They will not initiate hostilities, but they will defend themselves, the kingdom of Saudi Arabia, and other friends in the Persian Gulf."[22]

"A line has been drawn in the sand," the president said, but Saddam refused to cooperate.[23] Instead of invading Saudi Arabia and thus justifying an American declaration of war, the Iraqi army took a defensive stance in Kuwait. Unable to provoke Saddam into crossing the new line, Bush fell back on diplomacy, creating a broad international coalition dedicated to freeing Kuwait. He did so brilliantly, appealing to the Wilsonian principle of collective security and condemning the Iraqi action as a clear-cut case of aggression that threatened world peace.

His difficulty now became how best to persuade the American people to go beyond defending Saudi Arabia and to accept Operation Desert Storm, the use of armed force to liberate Kuwait. The president spoke in Wilsonian terms of "a new world order," and recalled the folly of 1930s appeasement, frequently equating Saddam with Hitler in trying to build a consensus for war.[24]

This emphasis on ideals obscured a fundamental national interest that clearly was involved. The Persian Gulf region was America's petroleum lifeline. After the sharp drop in the price of oil in the mid-1980s, American consumers began to dismiss the conservation efforts adopted during the 1970s energy crunch. As people drove larger, less fuel-efficient cars and used energy lavishly in pursuit of the good life, the nation once again became dependent on foreign oil for nearly half its consumption. The Persian Gulf, with 65 percent of the world's proven reserves and 25 percent of daily production, was vital to the U.S. economy. Saddam had done more than violate international law in seizing Kuwait; he had gained control of over 20 percent of the world's oil reserves and threatened a lion's share of the remainder. The American way of life as it had evolved in the course of the twentieth century—the reliance on the automobile, the sprawling suburbs, the vast interstate system, the vibrant Sun Belt dependent on air conditioning—was at stake in the Persian Gulf crisis.

President Bush felt he had to downplay this self-interested argument in order to appeal to world opinion, which would not be impressed with American domestic needs. When Secretary of State James Baker tried to be more candid, pointing out that "the economic lifeline of the industrial world runs from the Gulf," critics pounced when he added, "let me say that means jobs. If you want to sum it up in one word, its jobs." The ensuing outcry led to claims that the administration was willing to trade American lives to save a few cents at the gas pump, that "the vital interest at stake may be to make the world safe for gas guzzlers."[25]

In the face of this reaction, Bush could only intensify his idealistic rhetoric. He continued to compare Saddam to Hitler, even suggesting that "Saddam was the worse of the two," and called up the specter of Munich in condemning appeasement.[26] He reminded small nations of how dangerous it would be to allow Iraq to swallow up Kuwait. The appeal to collective security proved effective: It was a way to satisfy the international coalition and at the same time affirm traditional American ideals. But it left room for cynics to accuse Bush of using Wilsonian idealism to cloak less-exalted national interests.

There was one more drawback to Bush's efforts to justify the war: Excessive rhetoric led to excessive expectations. By picturing Saddam as such an evil leader, Bush led the American people to believe that the only satisfactory outcome of the war would be the destruction of his regime. Yet the very nature of the coalition, which included Arab members like Egypt and Syria, made it imperative to limit the war to the single announced goal of liberating Kuwait. By raising false expectations, Bush was creating a problem that would come back to haunt him at the war's end. I will return to that topic in the last chapter.

## American Exceptionalism

The American habit of refusing to fire the first shot, of drawing a line and then waiting to respond to an opponent's move, reflects a deeply ingrained national trait. I believe that it reflects a belief in American exceptionalism. Other nations go to war for narrow, selfish goals—for revenge, for territory, for economic gain, sometimes just out of a lust for world power. As citizens of a democracy, however, the American people view war as being justified only when it serves higher ends—when it advances the principles and values that lie at the core of the democratic experience.

A belief that the United States is exceptional—that it embodies virtues not found in other societies—finds expression in the concept of an American mission. It is America's role in the world to spread its values, such as respect for the individual and the right of self-government, for the benefit of all mankind. When Americans take up arms, it must be on behalf of these noble ideals.

The historical record reveals, however, that the United States goes to war for the same reasons as other nations—to protect and advance its own national interests. The nation fought in 1917 to protect its trade with the Allies and to preserve a favorable balance of power in Europe as well as to uphold the cause of democracy. It went to war in 1941 not just in self-defense after the Japanese attack on Pearl Harbor, but also to defeat a totalitarian threat to the American way of life. In Korea and Vietnam, although the United States advocated such principles as collective security and national self-determination, it fought primarily out of a misguided and distorted policy of trying to contain a worldwide Communist offensive. Finally, in the Persian Gulf, U.S. leaders invoked Wilsonian principles to justify their action when in reality the goal was to secure America's oil lifeline.

In short, throughout the twentieth century the American people believed they were fighting for principles rather than national self-interest. Most Americans see no contradiction between the assertion of ideals like collective security and self-government and the defense of American interests. What's good for the United States, to paraphrase Eisenhower's secretary of defense, Charles E. Wilson, is good for the world, and vice-versa. What Americans often fail to understand, however, is that others tend to view them as hypocrites, as people who proclaim crusades for right and freedom while advancing selfish national interests. Yet I believe that America's idealism is genuine, if sometimes misguided. Americans truly do see themselves, however reluctantly, as the world's best hope, and they are ready to rush in to help those in trouble—whether in Kuwait, Somalia, Haiti, Bosnia, or Kosovo—in places where others fear to tread. Such a willingness to answer the call of duty, to serve as the only nation responding to cries for help on the world's 911 system, indicates that the United States is indeed exceptional. Whatever their faults, the American people have been willing to engage in "perpetual war for perpetual peace" as long as they were convinced they were fulfilling their democratic mission.

# CHAPTER TWO

# Fighting Wars

Reluctant to take up arms, once engaged in war Americans seek to win them as quickly and as decisively as possible. Rather than viewing war as a natural, if unfortunate, aspect of human existence, they tend to see hostilities as painful interruptions in their usual way of life. They thus do everything possible to speed up the process so that they can return to what they consider the normal human condition, peacetime—or to refer again to Kennan's prehistoric monster, to sink blissfully back into the slime.

The way America goes to war does much to determine how it fights them. Seeking moral justifications for resorting to arms, Americans feel war must serve higher purposes than narrow national self-interest. By insisting on a moral purpose, by transforming conflicts into crusades, they tend to let their emotions dictate their actions. Instead of fighting for limited, tangible, achievable goals, Americans strive for lofty, often unattainable objectives. Thus Kennan notes "the difficulty we have in employing force for rational and restricted purposes rather than for purposes which are emotional and to which it is hard to find a rational limit."[1]

This was not always the case. In the nineteenth century, when America's power was clearly limited, the nation fought for more modest goals and was more easily satisfied. In 1846, although the United States ostensibly went to war to rebuff Mexican aggression, in fact it sought specific territory—especially California and the intervening province of New Mexico. After General Taylor defeated the enemy in northern Mexico, President Polk felt compelled to send Maj. Gen. Winfield Scott to capture Mexico City in an effort to compel Mexico to give America clear title to California and New Mexico. When Scott's control of the enemy's capital led a few eager expansionists to call for annexing all of Mexico, President Polk quickly limited American war aims to the northern provinces. He sought to fulfill America's manifest destiny by stretching its boundary to the Pacific; he had no interest in imperial rule over an alien country to the south.

In the Civil War, the North was equally clear about what it was fighting for. Lincoln resisted the calls of many to make the war a moral crusade to end slavery; he insisted from the outset that the sole purpose of fighting was to preserve the Union. When he did sign the Emancipation Proclamation, he viewed it as a wartime expedient, announcing only the freeing of slaves in the Confederacy and not in areas already controlled by the North. Lincoln ended the conflict when he achieved his objective of preserving the Union; freeing the slaves was but a by-product of that central goal.

America was equally single-minded in the war with Spain. Denouncing the brutal Spanish rule, it fought to free Cuba and end the atrocities there. The United States carefully renounced any effort to make Cuba an American colony; the goal was independence for the long-suffering people of Cuba. As soon as U.S. ground troops had defeated the Spanish outside Santiago and U.S. naval forces had sunk their fleet, America ended the fighting when Spain agreed to Cuban independence. It should be noted, however, that the nation satisfied its growing desire for overseas territory by acquiring Puerto Rico and the Philippines, and that it made the nominally independent Cuba an American protectorate with the Platt Amendment in 1902.

The nineteenth-century legacy was thus one of fighting for precise, clearly defined goals. Acutely aware of its limited power, America used force in a calculated fashion rather than engage in idealistic crusades. And it was successful, acquiring California and New Mexico, preserving the Union, and freeing Cuba in the process. Convinced of the rightness of its cause, America fought wars to advance its national interests.

In the twentieth century, however, the American attitude toward war would change; instead of fighting for specific national goals, Americans felt that only a higher cause could justify the material sacrifices and loss of life entailed in the mass slaughter made possible by modern weaponry. Yet Americans still expected wars to end in complete victory. As a result, the nation strove to fight total wars in hopes of achieving total peace. When the advent of the nuclear age made such an effort suicidal, America was compelled to revert to fighting limited wars for limited goals, and sometimes, as in Vietnam, failed even to achieve that modest objective.

## *The Wilsonian Imperative*

Wilson's proclamation of a great crusade in World War I marked a point of departure. Instead of fighting for such realistic aims as defending American rights on the high seas or preserving a favorable balance of power in Europe, Wilson persuaded the American people to fight for universal freedom and lasting world peace. His goal was to rise above the power politics that had led to an endless cycle of conflict and instead create a new international order in which nations great and small would band together to banish war forever.

Wilson's idealistic vision clashed sharply with the Allies's war aims. In the secret Treaty of London in 1915, England, France, Italy, and czarist Russia had agreed on how they would divide the spoils of war once the Central Powers were defeated—specifying the colonies, territory, and reparations each would demand from the vanquished. Suspecting such sordid objectives, Wilson was careful to keep the United States and its lofty goals separate and distinct from the Allies. He referred repeatedly to the "Allied and Associated Powers," making it clear that the United States was among the latter. When he agreed to send an American representative to the Supreme War Council in Paris, he insisted that cooperation be confined to coordinating the military effort and not extend to any plans for the future peace. "England and France," he commented to Col. Edward House, his most trusted diplomatic adviser, "*have not the same views with regard to peace that we have* by any means."[2]

Wilson's concern proved justified when the Bolsheviks revealed the terms of the Treaty of London in late 1917 to show the world the selfish motives of the capitalist nations in fighting the war. Although the president preferred to wait until the war was over to confront the Allies on the differences in war aims, he now felt compelled to speak out. On January 8, 1918, he gave a speech outlining his Fourteen Points for peace. He set forth several general principles to guide the future peacemakers, including freedom of the seas, removal of barriers to international trade, and the reduction of armaments, along with specific recommendations for the future map of Europe. The capstone was his plea for "a general association of nations . . . for the purpose of affording mutual guarantees of political independence and territorial integrity to great and small states alike."[3] Here was his boldest vision—he was advocating the principle of collective security to replace the discredited power politics of the past.

The Fourteen Points proved to be a masterful stroke of wartime psychology. The American president offered a rallying cry not only for his own people but for all mankind—the United States and, by association, the Allies, was fighting to free the world of the sins of militarism, imperialism, and the balance of power. He issued a call for a new international order based on freedom, justice, and equality among all nations. The Committee on Public Information, as the American wartime propaganda agency was known, quickly spread the Wilsonian message around the globe. More than 60 million pamphlets and leaflets carried the good news to people everywhere, among friend and foe alike, raising hopes that an Allied victory would usher in a new era of everlasting peace.

Wilson knew that by proclaiming his idealistic message he was insuring a bitter fight with the Allies when it came time to draw up the future peace. Nevertheless, he was confident that he had not only the support of the American people but of the common folk everywhere who were disgusted by the old order and ready to embrace the vision Wilson held out of a righteous and lasting peace.

The Fourteen Points thus became the heart of the Wilsonian crusade, giving body to his earlier call for a war to make the world safe for democracy. They helped to lift Allied morale and weaken the enemy's resolve. But they also reflected the arrogance of Wilson's conviction that he alone could change the course of history. After Germany's defeat, he discovered at the Paris peace conference just how hard it was to persuade the Allies to accept his vision. It proved far easier to call for a new international order than to create one out of the wreckage of the old. I will leave that story, however, for the final chapter.

## Unconditional Surrender

In the two decades following World War I, the American people reacted strongly against Wilson's idealism. When his vision failed to materialize, they felt betrayed and resolved never again to be seduced by dreams of a lasting peace. Disillusioned, they instead sought refuge in neutrality as Europe plunged toward war in the 1930s. This time, they vowed, the United States would stay out.

When the sense of national peril engendered by Nazi Germany's dramatic victories finally aroused the nation from its isolationist slumber, President Roosevelt carefully sought to avoid the mistakes of his Democratic predecessor. American security, not a new international order, became his focus in World War II.

The clearest sign of the new realism came with FDR's determination to make Germany's complete and utter defeat the nation's primary war aim. The resurgence of German militarism under Hitler convinced most Americans that it had been a mistake to fight for such unreachable goals as universal democracy and world peace. Instead of allowing Germany to sign an armistice and escape occupation, America would bring the war to the enemy's homeland and prevent Germany from ever again threatening the world's peace and stability. Roosevelt clearly had no intention of repeating Wilson's mistake of treating Germany with leniency.

Roosevelt chose the January, 1943, Casablanca conference with Churchill as the time to announce America's war objectives to the world. American and British forces had landed in North Africa in late 1942; at Casablanca, Churchill and Roosevelt agreed that once Africa was cleared of Axis forces, British and American troops should focus on the Mediterranean, invading Sicily and then Italy later in 1943. Although the two leaders privately agreed to continue plans for the eventual cross-channel invasion, they in effect were delaying D day until 1944. This postponement pained Gen. George C. Marshall, the U.S. Army chief of staff, and spelled trouble with the Soviet Union as FDR had promised Stalin a second front in western Europe before the end of 1942![4]

To Churchill's surprise, Roosevelt made a dramatic announcement at a press conference at the conclusion of the Casablanca conference. He told reporters that he and Churchill were determined "that peace can come to the world only by the total elimination of German and Japanese war power." Going on to cite the nickname of Civil War general "Unconditional Surrender" Grant, FDR declared: "The elimination of German, Japanese, and Italian war power means the unconditional surrender by Germany, Italy, or Japan." He added that it did not mean "the destruction of the population of Germany, Italy, and Japan" but only "the destruction of the philosophies in those countries which are based on conquest and the subjugation of other peoples."[5]

Unconditional surrender thus became America's avowed war aim in World War II. It served many useful purposes. It helped keep American morale high at a time when victories on the battlefield were few and far between. It promised a better world through the eventual elimination of evil regimes. Above all, it was designed to reassure the Soviets, who were engaged in a life-and-death struggle with the Germans at Stalingrad, deep within the Soviet Union.

Unconditional surrender also had its drawbacks, however. Critics pointed out that it helped Axis leaders rally their people, who, faced with no quarter from their opponents, would be more inclined to fight to the bitter end. Even more alarming was the simplistic notion that all the evil in the world resided in Germany and Japan, that once those aggressors were defeated, the American people could live in a world of peace and order. In that sense, unconditional surrender was like a magic elixir, promising a glorious peace without providing a blueprint or giving any details.

Above all, FDR's phrase revealed the inability of Americans to perceive the continuity between war and peace. The way the United States fought World War II was bound to shape the future peace. The defeat of Germany and Japan would not automatically lead to a world without conflict or tension. Churchill realized the real relationship between the military effort and the future shape of the world. That is why he resisted a cross-channel invasion and pressed instead for a strike northward from the Mediterranean. The soft underbelly of Europe might prove to be an illusion, as both American and British military strategists warned, but it offered a way to get Western forces into the heart of Europe ahead of the Red Army. Fearing a postwar clash with the Soviet Union for control of Europe, Churchill sought for ways to defeat Germany that would also enable

American and British troops to liberate as much of the continent as possible.

The gravest flaw in unconditional surrender was its failure to anticipate the vacuum of power that the total destruction of Germany and Japan would create in Europe and Asia. To fight solely for the defeat of the Axis nations was to ignore the realities of power and the strategic advantage enjoyed by the Soviet Union astride the center of the Eurasian landmass.

Concern over the implications of unconditional surrender led to a continuing Anglo-American debate over wartime strategy. Churchill lost out on his bid for a thrust up the Adriatic to accompany the cross-channel invasion. However, once British and American forces had liberated France, he renewed his efforts to gain control of as much of the continent as possible. When General Eisenhower chose a broad-front advance into Germany, Churchill objected. Backing Field Marshal Sir Bernard Law Montgomery, he called instead for a single thrust—a bold advance designed to get Western forces to Berlin ahead of the Soviets moving in from the east.

Military historians have long debated whether or not such an operation would have succeeded. Churchill's lament was that it never was given serious consideration. When Eisenhower rejected a strike on Berlin on military grounds, Churchill appealed to Washington, claiming it was a political decision. The death of Franklin Roosevelt meant that the new and inexperienced president, Harry Truman, had to decide. Truman referred the issue to Marshall, who quickly ruled out the strike against Berlin. As General Marshall later told Eisenhower, "Personally and aside from all logistical, tactical and strategical implications, I would be loath to hazard American lives for purely political purposes."[6]

Churchill was stunned. He believed in Carl von Clausewitz's dictum that war was the pursuit of political goals by other means. The Americans, in contrast, thought only of immediate victory, without considering the political consequences. One of Eisenhower's deputies, Gen. Omar N. Bradley, summed up the

American view: "As soldiers we looked naively on this British inclination to complicate the war with political foresight and non-military objectives."[7]

Unconditional surrender proved as unrealistic a war aim as Wilson's idealistic call to make the world safe for democracy. Although the United States achieved the total defeat of both Germany and Japan, victory produced not the peaceful world it expected, but rather the ominous peril of the Soviet Union controlling half of Europe and threatening the rest. Instead of the rosy future the American people had looked forward to as the reward for their wartime sacrifices, they were soon involved in the seemingly endless Cold War. The isolationist charge of "perpetual war for perpetual peace" seemed to be all too fitting a description of the outcome of World War II.

## Korea: The Perils of Limited War

The outbreak of fighting in Korea in June, 1950, quickly tested the American fondness for total war. In Europe, the policy of containment appeared to have succeeded in halting the Soviet threat to overrun the continent, but U.S. leaders feared that too great an involvement in Asia would leave America's North Atlantic Treaty Organization (NATO) allies exposed and vulnerable. The Russians had detonated their first atomic bomb in August, 1949, and while the United States maintained a strategic nuclear advantage, it now ran the risk of escalating local conflicts into a dreaded nuclear showdown with the Soviet Union. Moreover, Mao Tse-tung's victory in China had been a major setback, one that led the Republicans to accuse the Truman administration of failing to wage the Cold War effectively and allowed Sen. Joseph McCarthy to charge that the Democrats were soft on Communism.

Concerned over the impact of all-out war in Asia on America's vital European interests, yet fearful of Republican accusations of appeasement, Truman felt he had to fight a limited war in Korea. The original goal was simply to reestablish the border at the 38th Parallel by forcing North Korea back to that artificial boundary. General Douglas MacArthur's spectacular victory at Inch'on changed matters. By outflanking the North Koreans, who had been trying to drive American forces from the southern tip of the peninsula, MacArthur presented Truman with the possibility of transforming the conflict into a crusade to free Korea of Communism. It proved too tempting for Truman to resist. As North Korean forces fled northward in disorder, the president agreed with advisers who saw a chance to achieve a unified, non-Communist Korea and thus to capture what the Joint Chiefs of Staff referred to as "the eastern outpost of the iron curtain."[8] With congressional elections coming up within a few weeks, the president decided to preempt the Republicans by ordering an advance across the 38th Parallel.

The risks were enormous. Although the Soviet Union had not openly backed North Korea, an effort to overthrow a Russian-sponsored regime raised the possibility of either direct Soviet intervention, or more likely, action by its ally, Communist China. Moreover, as American troops approached the 38th Parallel, Beijing sent a warning via India that it was gravely concerned and would resist any U.S. effort to conquer North Korea. At home, others warned that if the United States became involved in a larger war with China, Western Europe would become an easy target for Soviet aggression.

Truman decided to move forward, but he and the Joint Chiefs carefully set up General MacArthur as the scapegoat if things should go wrong. Issuing highly ambiguous instructions, the Joint Chiefs authorized the supreme commander to cross the 38th Parallel to destroy North Korean forces as long as he did not perceive any danger of Soviet or Chinese intervention. If the Soviets acted, he was instructed to immediately assume a defensive posture. However, in the event of Chinese intervention, MacArthur was "to continue military action as long as it offered a reasonable chance of success."[9]

This was an extraordinary amount of discretion for a general well known for his impulsiveness. The administration clearly gave MacArthur free rein. George Marshall, whom Truman had just prevailed upon to serve as secretary of defense, confirmed this impression when he sent a personal message to the supreme commander, telling MacArthur that he should "feel unhampered tactically and strategically to proceed north of the 38th Parallel."[10]

The decision to abandon limited war and strive for a decisive victory in Korea led to a great debacle. It was fashionable at the time to blame MacArthur for what ensued, but in all fairness, President Truman and the Joint Chiefs were ultimately responsible. It is true that MacArthur brashly promised Truman at their famous meeting at Wake Island in October that the war would be over by Christmas. And MacArthur did commit a serious mistake by dividing his army and advancing to the Yalu River along the two coasts. Despite evidence of Chinese infiltration as early as late October, MacArthur pursued a reckless course that proved disastrous in late November when hundreds of thousands of Chinese troops overwhelmed the divided American columns. Once again Communist forces swept down the Korean peninsula, recapturing Seoul and leading Washington to consider complete evacuation to Japan before the new field commander, Gen. Matthew B. Ridgway, was able to halt the onslaught in early 1951.

Chastened by this humiliating setback, Truman and his advisers gave up plans for unifying Korea and decided to settle for a cease-fire restoring the prewar status quo. By March, Ridgway had recaptured Seoul and established a defensive line near the 38th Parallel. However, back in Tokyo, MacArthur seethed at the new policy of accepting a stalemate in Korea. Emboldened by the discretion he had been given earlier, he proposed attacking China and even called on Beijing to surrender or face destruction. Truman tried to reassert his authority but MacArthur then went too far. In late March, the supreme commander sent a reply to a Republican congressional leader in which he criticized his superiors in Washington for subordinating Asia to Europe, asserting: "It seems strangely difficult for some to realize that here in Asia is where the Communist conspirators have elected to make their play for global conquest . . . ; that here we fight Europe's war with arms while the diplomats still fight it with words; that if we lose this war to Communism in Asia the fall of Europe is inevitable." The Republican leader then made MacArthur's insubordinate message public, complete with its defiant conclusion that "There is no substitute for victory."[11]

Truman fired MacArthur a week later. In the storm of public controversy that ensued, the president's popularity fell below 25 percent in the polls. But even Republican critics found it difficult to excuse MacArthur's violation of the basic principle of civilian control of the military. Moreover, Secretary of Defense George Marshall and General Bradley, chairman of the Joint Chiefs of Staff, spelled out the global considerations that had led them to advise Truman to forego victory in Korea. Marshall warned that MacArthur's strategy not only risked war with both China and the Soviet Union but that it would also lead to "losing our allies and wrecking the coalition of free peoples throughout the world." Bradley was more succinct, pointing out that the Joint Chiefs had "global responsibilities" that outweighed the parochial views of "a theater commander." MacArthur's plans, he concluded, would put the United States "in the wrong war, at the wrong place, at the wrong time and with the wrong enemy."[12]

Although Truman never regained the public's confidence, the American people accepted Marshall's and Bradley's military judgment and allowed MacArthur to "just fade away—an old soldier who tried to do his duty as God gave him the light to see that duty."[13]

Above all else, the Korean War showed that the American habit of fighting for total victory had become a casualty of the nuclear age. In the global contest with the Soviet Union, limited war made much greater sense, both in terms of geographical priorities and the need to avoid direct confrontation between the superpowers. While MacArthur was wrong, it was the

Truman administration that bore most of the responsibility for the outcome. Having given MacArthur far too much discretion, the president and the Joint Chiefs could hardly have been surprised when he resisted their efforts to restrain him. It was the men in Washington who had changed the original war aim from defending the 38th Parallel to attempting to unify Korea. Had Truman and his advisers not been tempted by MacArthur's success at Inch'on, they might have been able to end the war before Christmas, 1950, and spared the nation and themselves much grief.

## Vietnam: All-out Limited War

Vietnam posed an even more difficult challenge to the American belief that the object of war is the enemy's complete and total defeat. Unlike Korea, the problem was not an unwise attempt to use force to unify a divided nation. Instead the difficulty stemmed from pursuing an impossible goal: fighting a war to preserve the artificial division of Vietnam in the face of Hanoi's determination to achieve national unity.

The American strategic dilemma in Vietnam stemmed directly from the nation's ambivalent war aims. Unsure whether the United States was fighting simply to defend South Vietnam, to halt a Communist threat to all Southeast Asia (the domino theory), or just to honor past commitments, Lyndon Johnson and his civilian advisers failed to give the military a clear-cut objective. The result was a strategic vacuum that helps explain why the Vietnamese David was able to bring down the American Goliath.

Having inherited the dreaded Queen of Spades, LBJ was determined not to do two things in Vietnam. The first, based on the Korean experience, was not to expand the conflict by involving China. Determined to carry out his Great Society program at home, the president was insistent on limiting the war in Vietnam. At the same time, recalling the impact of the so-called loss of China on the Democratic Party, he was equally intent on not withdrawing, telling Richard Russell that the American people would "impeach a President . . . that would run out."[14] He thus ended up with a policy of fighting to defend the status quo. Under LBJ, the preservation of an independent South Vietnam became America's strategic goal.

The great tragedy that ensued was due largely to LBJ's ego. Seeking a limited objective, he was nonetheless so determined to achieve it that he was willing to use virtually unlimited force—to engage in what Assistant Secretary of State William Bundy termed an "all-out limited war." The result, in the words of historian George Herring, was "a huge, sprawling, many-faceted, military-civilian effort, generally uncoordinated, in which, all too frequently, the various components worked against rather than in support of each other."[15]

The primary goal of America's military policy in Vietnam was to inflict enough pain and suffering on the Communist opponents to force them to end their attempts to subvert the government of South Vietnam. The United States used vast amounts of airpower, both to bomb military targets in the north and in support of ground operations in the south. Although America dropped more bombs on Vietnam than it did in all of World War II, it still failed to halt the infiltration of North Vietnamese reinforcements and supplies to the Vietcong, and only hardened Hanoi's determination to hold out until the United States became frustrated and left. North Vietnam was also able to use the U.S. bombing campaign to elicit world sympathy for the plight of its people.

On the ground, a policy of attrition proved equally bankrupt. Johnson allowed Gen. William C. Westmoreland to pursue a "search and destroy" strategy to achieve the goal of defending South Vietnam. Westmoreland followed traditional U.S. Army doctrine—use superior firepower to wear down the enemy. "They had to be pounded with artillery and bombs and eventually brought to battle on the ground," he later wrote of the North Vietnamese forces, "if they were not forever to remain a threat."[16] But the enemy refused to cooperate. They used hit-and-run tactics and drew U.S. forces deep into the interior, where the terrain and shorter supply lines favored them. By the end of 1967, the United States had nearly half a million men in Vietnam and had achieved only a bloody stalemate. It had prevented the enemy from conquering South Vietnam, but in the process had destroyed much of the countryside and suffered heavy casualties. One of Johnson's advisers, Undersecretary of State Nicholas Katzenbach, made an apt comparison: "Hanoi uses time the way Russians used terrain before Napoleon's advance on Moscow, always retreating, losing every battle, but eventually creating conditions in which the enemy can no longer function. For Napoleon it was his long supply lines and the cold Russian winter; Hanoi hopes that for us it will be the mounting dissension, impatience, and frustration caused by a protracted war without fronts or other visible signs of success."[17]

Hanoi calculated correctly; by 1967 it was the American home front that cracked. Murmurs of dissent that started on college campuses with "teach-ins" began to spread as every night the evening news showed American troops waging a bloody war with an unseen enemy on unfamiliar terrain. Nationally televised hearings by the Senate Foreign Relations Committee helped make protest against the war respectable; soon Johnson could not travel across the land without facing mobs of angry demonstrators. He spoke of being trapped in the White House, "like a jackrabbit hunkered up in a storm."[18] His wife gave an even more apt description. "A miasma of trouble hangs over everything," Lady Bird Johnson wrote in her diary in early 1967. "The temperament of our people seems to be, 'you must either get excited, get passionate, fight and get it over with, or we must pull out.' It is unbearably hard to fight a limited war."[19]

The Tet offensive a year later proved just how hard it was. Although the Vietcong uprising in cities across South Vietnam caught the American military by surprise, U.S. and South Vietnamese troops quickly regained control of most urban areas, except for Hue, where the fighting went on for several weeks.

They inflicted heavy casualties on the Vietcong, thereby weakening their control of the countryside and allowing the Pentagon to claim an impressive military victory. But to the rest of the world, and above all to the American people, the dramatic attack, especially on the U.S. embassy compound in Saigon, was a devastating psychological blow. It contradicted all the rosy statements Johnson and Westmoreland had made about the prospects for victory. When all the military could propose after this supposed triumph was to ask for two hundred thousand more combat troops, Lyndon Johnson was compelled to begin reassessing the war. Realizing that it was no longer possible to continue defending South Vietnam without risking political defeat at home, Johnson began the slow process of withdrawal on March 31 by announcing his decision not to run for reelection.

The question that still haunts the American conscience is whether or not the United States could have won the Vietnam War. After America's humiliating withdrawal in the 1970s, prominent military spokesmen and their supporters, most notably Col. Harry Summers, charged that the armed forces never had a chance. The middle course that Johnson insisted upon tied their hands. Had the generals been given free rein, the revisionists claim, America could have carried the war home to the enemy, invading North Vietnam and using superior U.S. weaponry to force Hanoi to surrender. While these critics do not claim that the United States should have used nuclear weapons to achieve this goal, they feel it was a mistake to rule them out. In early 1968, Westmoreland had begun a secret study of how tactical nuclear warheads might be used to defend the besieged garrison at Khe Sanh, but LBJ ordered him to cancel it. "I felt at the time and even more so now," Westmoreland wrote in his memoirs, "that to fail to consider this alternative was a mistake."[20] Summers argues that America's revulsion at the thought of nuclear war "cost us a major strategic advantage— . . . the ability to pose a threat to the enemy to raise the level of warfare beyond his ability (or willingness) to respond."[21]

It is to Lyndon Johnson's everlasting credit that he never gave serious consideration to using nuclear weapons to resolve the Vietnam dilemma. His entire approach to the war was based on the desire to limit the conflict to Vietnam and not allow it to escalate by involving China and the Soviet Union. In making it clear to his generals that "all-out limited war" did not include nuclear weapons, LBJ acted not only morally but wisely.

It retrospect, it is clear why America lost in Vietnam. The United States failed to bring its ends and means into a reasonable balance. If the goal had been victory at any cost then the revisionists are right—America could have won the war. But the means necessary to achieve that objective would have made sense only if it had been trying to unify all Vietnam under a non-Communist government. Instead of using more force to defend South Vietnam, Johnson would have been wiser to have used less, adopting an enclave strategy in South Vietnam and using air strikes against the north in a more limited and precise way. Yet even if America's use of force had been restricted to fit better with the limited strategic goal of simply defending South Vietnam, it would not have succeeded. The force of nationalism, coupled with Hanoi's determination to wait the United States out, eventually would have made America give up a hopeless task. Limited war can only be fought successfully if the goals are both clearly defined and within reasonable reach. In Vietnam, America used virtually unlimited means in pursuit of an unrealistic end; it is hardly surprising that the nation's efforts resulted in failure.

## An Incomplete Success

The United States did a better job of adjusting means to fit the ends in the Persian Gulf War. Like Korea, it was a coalition effort, but unlike Korea, more than just in name. President Bush, who had worked hard to forge an international response to Iraq's invasion of Kuwait, had to keep the coalition's fragile makeup constantly in mind while fighting the war. In advocating the use of force on behalf of collective security, Bush focused on the common goal: to liberate Kuwait and prove to the world that aggression did not pay.

The nature of the coalition placed clear limits on the U.S. war effort. There was no basic conflict with America's prime national security interest: protecting the Persian Gulf oil lifeline. The massive buildup of American forces in Saudi Arabia in the fall of 1990, Operation Desert Shield, had already achieved that goal; Operation Desert Storm, the liberation of Kuwait, would advance it further. The problem Bush faced was of his own making. By demonizing Saddam Hussein, he created an expectation among the American people that the war would topple the Iraqi dictator. In fighting the war, the president had to find a way to keep the traditional American desire for total victory from disrupting the coalition's effort to achieve the limited aim of liberating Kuwait.

The Bush administration relied on a twofold military strategy. First, it planned to use airpower to soften up Iraq through extensive aerial bombardment aimed primarily at strategic targets—especially the air defense network and the command and control system whereby Saddam in Baghdad communicated his orders to commanders in the field. In addition, the air campaign sought to cripple Iraq's infrastructure by targeting bridges and roads as well as power plants and water systems. At the army's insistence, the air force also sought to weaken the enemy's armed forces with attacks on tank formations and on the troops dug in to defend Kuwait. But this tactical use of airpower was always considered secondary to the strategic effort to destroy the enemy's ability to wage war.

Although some air force planners thought that airpower alone could determine the outcome, Gen. Colin L. Powell, chairman of the Joint Chiefs of Staff, and Gen. H. Norman Schwarzkopf, the theater commander, believed that victory could only come through a massive ground assault. Powell put it most starkly when he told a press conference in January, 1991, that America's strategy for attacking Saddam's army was "very simple. . . . First, we are going to cut it off, and then we are going to kill it."[22] In Saudi Arabia, Schwarzkopf saw the air assault as similar to artillery barrages in earlier wars: It was designed to soften up the enemy before the infantry attacked. The ground offensive would feature a feint at the center to disguise the main blow—a vast envelopment from the left flank designed to trap Iraq's best troops, the Republican Guard, when they advanced from southern Iraq to counter the U.S. attack on Kuwait. American armed forces, primarily the VII Corps, recently transferred from Germany—where it had remained throughout the Cold War, ready to defend against a Soviet attack on central Europe—would sweep across the desert to surround and destroy the Republican Guard and the rest of the Iraqi armed forces. This bold plan would enable the United States to achieve the coalition's goal of liberating Kuwait while at the same time fulfilling Bush's hope of undermining Saddam by destroying the Republican Guard.

The twofold American plan for an aerial softening up of Iraq followed by a lightning ground assault designed both to free Kuwait and cripple Saddam's regime proved only partially successful. The air war, while effective and at times spectacular, had its limitations. One was the Scud problem. Saddam began firing Scud missiles at cities in Saudi Arabia and Israel. Although they are primitive weapons with limited range and poor accuracy, the Scuds were highly effective politically. Bush and his advisers were particularly concerned about the Israeli reaction. When Arab members threatened to pull out of the coalition if Israel entered the conflict, the United States had to exert considerable diplomatic pressure on the Israelis to keep them from retaliating against Iraq.

To counter the Scud threat, the United States sent Patriot missile batteries to both Saudi Arabia and Israel. The highly touted Patriots scored few hits on the Scuds but they did provide valuable political reassurance. Meanwhile, the air force engaged in what journalists termed the "Great Scud Hunt."[23] Planes were diverted from their planned targets to search for

Scud launchers in Iraq's vast desert regions. Despite using more than one-fourth of its available aircraft, the air force succeeded only in knocking out dummy launchers. After the war, intelligence experts learned that U.S. planes had failed to destroy a single one of the elusive mobile Scud launchers in Iraq.

A postwar *Washington Post* analysis also showed that U.S. air attacks on Baghdad were much less effective than the public was led to believe. Despite some spectacular successes, most notably the film clip of a laser-guided bomb entering an airshaft and destroying the Iraqi air force headquarters, the destruction in Baghdad was quite limited. In fact, the air force targeted only a few key government buildings in an effort to avoid civilian casualties. Just 244 laser-guided bombs and eighty-eight cruise missiles, less than 3 percent of all such "smart" weapons used in Desert Storm, hit the Iraqi capital.[24] As a result, the United States was unable to cripple Saddam's ability to rule or to control his forces in battle. Moreover, despite concentrating on military targets, there was extensive collateral damage—the destruction of a "baby milk" factory, the death of hundreds of civilians in the Amiriya air raid shelter, and the extensive suffering that resulted from the destruction of Iraq's power grid and utility systems.

The ground war, though very successful, also did not go quite according to plan. Schwarzkopf had hoped that the Marine Corps attack on the center would draw the Republican Guard into Kuwait, allowing Saddam's elite forces to be trapped by American armored units racing across the desert. But the general failed to reckon with the Marine Corps's determination to fight more than a holding action. Instead, following their own timetable, the marines smashed through the Iraqi defenses and fought their way to the outskirts of Kuwait City in just three days. Military commentators Michael Gordon and Gen. Bernard Trainor pointed out that "the Marines had routed the Iraqis so quickly that the Army had not yet built up a head of steam for what was to be the main attack."[25] By the time VII Corps crossed the desert into southern Iraq, Saddam, realizing that Kuwait was lost, had ordered the Republican Guard to retreat across the Euphrates to protect Baghdad.

This unexpected development created a genuine dilemma for President Bush and General Powell in Washington. How could they pursue the plan to cripple Saddam by destroying the Republican Guard when they had already achieved the coalition's primary goal, the liberation of Kuwait? I will leave that issue to the final chapter since it relates to the way America has ended its wars.

By any reasonable standard, the United States had been remarkably successful in achieving its stated goals in the Persian Gulf War. It had put together a broad international coalition and maintained it effectively, keeping Israel out of the conflict and even holding back the marines on the outskirts of Kuwait City to allow Egyptian, Saudi, and other Arab troops to march triumphantly into that key objective. It had demonstrated the effectiveness of airpower in weakening the enemy and permitting the ground offensive to be so swift and relatively bloodless. At the same time, in defending Saudi Arabia and restoring Kuwait, it had served U.S. national interests by guaranteeing Americans continued access to the world's richest supply of oil.

Yet, in the words of Gordon and Trainor, it was at best only "an incomplete success."[26] The American people felt disappointed that U.S. forces had failed to drive Saddam Hussein from power. President Bush had succeeded in fighting a coalition war while holding in check the traditional American desire for total victory, but he shared a sense of inadequacy at his inability to bring down the man he had compared to Adolf Hitler. The initial wave of euphoria over the decisive victory in the desert war, obliterating as it did the legacy of defeat in Vietnam, ultimately gave way to growing disillusionment with the outcome.

## Conclusion

The American desire to fight wars to fulfill a high moral purpose clashed with the realities of world politics in the twentieth century. Americans have failed to understand the continuity between war and peace—that resorting to arms is but another way to advance national interests. Viewing war as an unnatural state and peace as the norm, Americans were constantly forgetting that the way they fought a war had a lasting impact on the peace that followed. Even though the United States won most of the wars it fought in the twentieth century, with the important exception of Vietnam, the nation emerged from those conflicts dissatisfied and unfulfilled. Believing that victory would lead to a better and more peaceful world, Americans were chagrined to find themselves still living in a dangerous and unpredictable international arena.

In World War I, Wilson's belief that defeating Germany would lead to a new international order based on peace and justice clashed with the Allies' determination to gain the spoils of war. Instead of enjoying the lasting peace promised by Wilson, Americans found themselves involved in a second global conflict just two decades later. In World War II, Roosevelt's insistence on unconditional surrender helped create a power vacuum in the aftermath of the total defeat of Germany and Japan. In an effort to prevent the Soviet Union from filling that vacuum, the United States embarked on the Cold War. The fear of direct confrontation with the Soviets in the nuclear age forced America to fight limited wars. In Korea, America learned the hard way the need to give up its national habit of striving for total victory. In Vietnam, the nation's own ambivalent war aims, together with the powerful force of Vietnamese nationalism, led to a humiliating defeat. Even the Gulf War, an apparent triumph of American arms, proved frustrating as the United States successfully upheld the principle of collective security in liberating Kuwait but failed to drive Saddam from power because of the need for coalition diplomacy.

As a people, Americans have tended to go to war with unrealistic expectations. They view war as an unnatural state; a departure from the normal peacetime condition that could only be justified by a high and noble purpose. Their inability to see war as simply a way to fulfill America's national interests when peaceful diplomacy fails has clouded their judgment and repeatedly led to postwar disillusionment. This tendency has had its greatest impact on the final stages of America's involvement in twentieth-century wars—on the way U.S. leaders sought to end conflicts and make peace. I will explore that topic in the last chapter.

CHAPTER THREE

# Ending Wars

As a nation, the United States has had more difficulty ending wars than in either entering into or fighting them. The problem often stemmed from the failure to define clear-cut and realistic war aims. The belief that resorting to arms could only be justified in terms of broad ideals made it difficult for the nation's leaders to end the conflicts without realizing these exalted goals.

As we have already seen, the American belief that peace is the normal human condition and war an aberration helped compound the difficulty. Americans failed to realize the continuity between war and peace and the fact that the way they waged war was bound to influence the peace that followed. Instead, they tended to think that resorting to arms would resolve the issues that had led them to war in the first place and would usher in a new era of tranquillity.

In the nineteenth century, even though the nation's goals were more limited, Americans still experienced problems ending wars in a way that seemed to justify their high cost in lives and resources. The most startling exception was the War of 1812. The United States went to war with England ostensibly to defend its neutral rights during the Napoleonic Wars, invoking the principle of freedom of the seas to contest British maritime practices such as blockade and impressment. In reality, America fought primarily out of frustration and a desire to defend the national honor. The war went badly: U.S. troops failed to conquer Canada, and the nation had to endure the British raid on Washington and the burning of the White House. American diplomats, led by John Quincy Adams, did well to negotiate a peace that ignored all the issues that had led to war and simply ended the fighting. Yet news of Andrew Jackson's victory at New Orleans, in a battle fought after the signing of the Treaty of Ghent, persuaded the American people that they had forced Britain to end the hostilities. The outcome of what some termed the Second War for American Independence contradicted the old American adage that the United States always wins the war and loses the peace. In this case, it lost the war to a far more powerful adversary but won the peace by escaping with its territory intact.

The war with Mexico also ended strangely. In this case, the difficulty was not winning on the battlefield but rather finding a Mexican government willing to legitimize America's wartime conquests. After General Scott occupied Mexico City, President Polk sent an obscure diplomat, Nicholas Trist, to negotiate a treaty transferring sovereignty over California and New Mexico to the United States. Irritated by Trist's failure to act quickly, as well as by his long and tedious dispatches, Polk ordered him home. But Trist, finally making headway in Mexico City, sent back a sixty-five-page letter rejecting the president's order and then proceeded to achieve precisely what Polk wanted in the Treaty of Guadalupe Hidalgo. Under its terms the United States acquired legal title to California and New Mexico, as well as the Rio Grande boundary for Texas, for just over $18 million. Polk responded ungraciously by denouncing Trist, who had to wait twenty-two years before Congress paid him for his services. But the president accepted the treaty and quickly submitted it to the Senate. One critic aptly summed up the outcome by commenting that the peace "negotiated by an unauthorized agent, with an unacknowledged government, submitted by an accidental president, to a dissatisfied Senate, has, notwithstanding these objections in form, been confirmed."[1]

Lincoln was able to achieve his principal war aim in the Civil War when Gen. Robert E. Lee surrendered unconditionally to Grant. The South's attempts to gain independence failed and the Union was preserved.

The war with Spain a generation later ended more ambiguously. The United States, after the landings in Cuba and the destruction of the Spanish fleet off Santiago, achieved its primary war aim of ending Spanish rule in Cuba. But the island was not yet completely free. American troops occupied Cuba for nearly four years and left only after Cuban officials agreed to the terms of the Platt Amendment, making the island an American protectorate.

It is also worth noting that while the United States lived up to its pledge not to annex Cuba, it used the war to acquire the Philippines, another Spanish possession halfway around the globe. On the pretext of neutralizing the Spanish Pacific fleet, President McKinley, with help from Assistant Secretary of the Navy Theodore Roosevelt, ordered Commodore George Dewey to Manila Bay. After Dewey destroyed the Spanish squadron there on May 1, 1898, McKinley sent army forces to occupy Manila. Even though the city had not fallen when the armistice was signed in August, U.S. diplomats forced Spain to transfer title to the archipelago in the Treaty of Paris ending the war. In return, the United States paid Spain $20 million and was soon forced to send out more troops and engage in brutal counterinsurgency measures to defeat the outraged Filipinos.

The relatively brief and bloodless Spanish-American War had far-reaching consequences. Fighting ostensibly for humanitarian reasons, the United States emerged from the conflict as a world power. It had defeated a European nation, gained territory across the Pacific, and apparently had given the world notice that it would be a force to be reckoned with in the international arena. The nation that had fought its earlier wars for limited, specific ends was now ready to seek broader goals on the world stage.

# The Great Betrayal?

As we have seen, Woodrow Wilson insisted on making the American effort in World War I a crusade for a better world. For Wilson, the war itself was but the prelude to the peace that would follow. The loss of American lives would be justified by repudiating the old balance-of-power system and replacing it with a new one devoted to justice and the equality of all nations.

Wilson showed his determination to achieve a just peace in the fall of 1918 when German power was crumbling. The Allies wanted to occupy Germany and humiliate their enemy, but when Berlin indicated a willingness to sue for peace based on the Fourteen Points, Wilson insisted on negotiating the armistice. By that time, more than a million American troops were fighting in Europe and the United States had the power to force the war-weary Allies to accede to its demands.

Wilson then faced two great obstacles in his quest for a just and lasting peace. The first was the Allies' determination to resist his call for a peace of reconciliation and to try to gain the spoils of war at the Paris peace conference. Wilson insisted that the victors make a world organization both an integral part of the peace settlement and the first order of business. When the Allies reluctantly accepted the covenant of the new League of Nations in January, 1919, it appeared that the American idealist had triumphed over the European realists.

Over the next several months, however, Wilson was forced to fight a bitter battle with Georges Clemenceau of France and David Lloyd George of Britain. He won some of the skirmishes, insisting on the principle of national self-determination in settling territorial issues and accepting the mandate system as a compromise on the disposition of colonial claims.

But he lost others. Clemenceau held out on the Rhineland, determined to do all he could to prevent a future German invasion by holding on as long as possible to a strategic bit of German territory in violation of national self-determination. Most serious of all, Wilson gave way on the issue of reparations, allowing the Allies to use the loophole of veterans' pensions to expand the amount of civilian damages in the bill they presented to Germany. The sum eventually grew to $33 billion, far beyond Germany's capacity to pay. Onerous reparations, together with a war guilt clause to justify them, robbed the eventual Treaty of Versailles of any pretense to being the peace without victory that Wilson desired. It was instead a vindictive treaty, harsh enough to stimulate the German desire for revenge but not punitive enough to prevent the future revival of German military power. Rather than leading to a lasting peace, the Treaty of Versailles simply ushered in a twenty-year armistice separating the twentieth century's world wars.

Wilson knew the peace was flawed but he felt confident that his beloved League of Nations would provide a forum to address all postwar problems and enable the world to settle them peacefully. It was the second obstacle, the U.S. Senate's refusal to ratify his handiwork, that destroyed his dream of a new world order.

The struggle over the ratification of the Treaty of Versailles has often been portrayed as a contest between strong-willed individuals: Woodrow Wilson, intent on American leadership in the League of Nations; Sen. Henry Cabot Lodge, equally determined to limit future American commitments; and Sen. William Borah, willing to fight to the end to preserve traditional American isolationism. But the struggle involved more than personalities. There was genuine disagreement over the principle of collective security. Wilson insisted that peace was indivisible—the United States could not be secure unless it opposed aggression everywhere. Borah believed it was in the national interest to resist all foreign involvement. Lodge, never an isolationist, took the middle ground, ready to cooperate as a League member but always insisting that the United States be free to act in its own best interest and not automatically engage in collective peace efforts.

Wilson's refusal to compromise doomed his grand hopes for peace. The United States, critics have charged, could have joined the League if Wilson had only accepted Lodge's reservations, giving the United States the veto power that it would later insist upon in the future United Nations. Yet Wilson was right not to give way. He saw that the only way that collective security could spare the world future wars would be if the United States embraced it wholeheartedly and completely. Pressed by Lodge, he admitted that the obligation the United States assumed in embracing collective security was not just a legal one, but a moral imperative. When wrongdoing occurred, America would lead the world community in stopping it and restoring peace. "There is only one power to put behind the liberation of mankind," Wilson declared, "and that is the power of mankind. It is the power of the united moral forces of the world, and in the covenant of the League of Nations the moral forces of the world are mobilized."[2] If Americans were not willing to accept that moral obligation, then Wilson believed it would be better to decline to join than to mislead the world. In other words, Wilson sincerely felt that anything less than full commitment would amount to collective insecurity.

In *Woodrow Wilson and the Great Betrayal,* Thomas Bailey described Wilson's refusal to compromise as "the supreme act of infanticide."[3] Without the United States, the League of Nations was bound to fail. Yet I would argue that Wilson was right to insist on all or nothing. As the subsequent experiment in collective security, the United Nations, has demonstrated, it is nearly impossible for nations to rise above their own national interests to act together for world peace. It is doubtful that the League would have been any more effective in dealing with Japanese aggression in Manchuria in 1931 or the Italian invasion of Ethiopia in 1935 with the United States an active member, given the mood of isolationism that prevailed in the 1930s. No one was betrayed in 1919, nor was any baby killed when the Senate rejected the Treaty of Versailles to avoid joining the League of Nations. Instead, the Senate vote reflected the prevailing view of the American people. Wilson had asked them to embrace wholeheartedly and without reservation the principle of collective security. They preferred to continue to place their trust in more traditional ways of promoting and protecting the national interest.

## Ending World War II

Franklin Roosevelt viewed World War II in just the opposite fashion from Woodrow Wilson. Where Wilson believed the war was but the prelude to his effort to fashion a just and lasting peace, FDR concentrated on winning the war itself, in the hope that the defeat of the Axis powers would automatically lead to a better world. He preferred to postpone all political issues to the postwar period in order to prevent them from becoming obstacles to the victory he so single-mindedly sought.

There was one exception. Intent on achieving the goal that had eluded Wilson, FDR made American leadership in founding a new world organization a top wartime priority. However, the world body that Roosevelt envisioned was a far cry from the Wilsonian League of Nations. Instead of basing it on the equality of all nations, FDR tried to preserve the concept of power embodied in the wartime coalition. The four nations that had led the fight against the Axis—the United States, Great Britain, the Soviet Union, and China—would become the Four Policemen that would dominate the future United Nations. Since the Soviet Union was equally intent on preserving its freedom of action, the United States had no difficulty persuading the San Francisco conference to adopt a charter for the UN that gave the Four Policemen, along with France, the veto power they needed to protect their own national interests.

Aside from the United Nations, the policy of unconditional surrender worked well in focusing attention on winning the war and postponing issues relating to the future peace. In Italy, after Benito Mussolini was forced out of power in the summer of 1943, the few minor concessions the United States and Britain made to ensure Italian military cooperation were rendered meaningless by the quick German advance to Rome. Roosevelt and Churchill kept the occupation and liberation of Italy an Anglo-American monopoly, and the Russians responded with only a token protest. They saw in Italy a useful precedent for their later exclusion of the Western powers from Eastern Europe.

The German surrender followed the unconditional surrender formula almost to the letter. Although some German leaders sought to surrender in the west while still fighting the Russians in the east, the only early surrender came in Italy in early May. In Germany, Eisenhower kept the Soviets fully informed and would accept only a complete and total German capitulation. Despite this cooperation, it was another month before the Soviets allowed British and American occupation forces to join them in Berlin.

It was the end of the Pacific War that provided the most serious challenge to the unconditional surrender formula. President Truman, who succeeded Roosevelt after his death in April, faced a genuine problem in achieving the surrender of an already defeated Japan.

Japan was in a precarious position by the summer of 1945. The Japanese had lost the bulk of their navy in a futile defense of the Philippines and American B-29s were firebombing Japanese cities with impunity. In just five days in March, 1945, incendiary attacks had devastated much of Tokyo and caused nearly a hundred thousand deaths. Yet Japan still had 5 million men under arms and controlled much of Asia, from Korea and China in the north to Burma and Indonesia in the south. The U.S. invasion of Okinawa in the spring had shown how dangerous Japan could be. More than thirteen thousand Americans died in the savage fighting on the island, and Japanese kamikazes sank twenty-seven American warships offshore.

President Truman and his advisers had to choose among three alternatives for forcing Japan to surrender. The first, planned by the military throughout the war, was to invade the Japanese home islands. The Pentagon's plans called for two amphibious landings. The first, code-named Operation Olympic, was a ten-division assault on the southernmost island of Kyushu, scheduled for November, 1945. The final attack, Operation Coronet, slated for March, 1946, called for twenty-five divisions, many fresh from the European theater, to land on Honshu and fight the final battle on the Tokyo plain.

There is a scholarly debate over the number of casualties the United States expected to suffer in these operations. After the war, estimates given by President Truman and Secretary of War Henry Stimson ranged from 250,000 to 1 million killed and wounded. At the time, General MacArthur believed that the attack on Kyushu might result in 100,000 casualties. Pentagon planners, who thought that the Japanese would surrender after they lost Kyushu, estimated the battle deaths at between 15,000 and 30,000—not that much more than the 13,000 Americans who died invading Okinawa or the 16,000 on the beaches of Normandy.

Whatever the numbers, Truman was understandably determined to do all he could to avoid the loss of a single additional American life. Undersecretary of State Joseph Grew, the prewar U.S. ambassador to Japan, offered a way to achieve that goal by diplomacy. He urged that Truman depart from the unconditional surrender formula in just one important way: allow the Japanese to retain their emperor. Hirohito, he pointed out, was only a figurehead. However, despite his lack of power, the Japanese regarded the emperor as a deity; sparing him would give Japanese political leaders a way to give up graciously.

The problem lay with American wartime views of Japan. The United States had portrayed Hirohito as a villain, a personification of evil like Hitler and Mussolini. The new secretary of state, James Byrnes, warned Truman that if he appeared to let Hirohito escape punishment, he would lose the trust of the American people. A naval officer, fearful of just such a move, expressed a widespread feeling when he warned that failing to remove the emperor "means a short-of-victory war with Japan—and that, in turn, means another war with Japan" in the future.[4]

President Truman rejected Grew's suggestion and instead followed Byrnes's advice in issuing the Potsdam Declaration. He called on Japan to surrender, promising not to enslave the Japanese nor abolish their nation. But he was silent on the key question of the emperor. When the Japanese government gave an ambiguous reply, Truman felt he had no choice but to proceed with the third alternative.

The decision to use the recently completed atomic bomb made good sense from Truman's perspective. A war-weary American public would never have condoned not using a weapon that promised to end the conflict quickly and without the loss of additional American lives. The ensuing atomic destruction of Hiroshima and Nagasaki proved effective. By mid-August, Hirohito felt compelled to break with tradition and enter into the political process to arrive at the decision to surrender unconditionally.

Ever since, critics have claimed that Truman made a mistake in using the atomic bomb. Some argue that the Soviet Union's entry into the war on August 8, just as promised at Yalta, would have been enough to bring about Japan's surrender. Others claim that continued conventional bombing as well as a tightened naval blockade would have forced Tokyo to give in long before the scheduled assault on Kyushu in November. We will never know if these skeptics are right. The fact remains that Truman used the bomb, which in turn brought about a rapid Japanese surrender.

The tragedy lies in Truman's unwillingness to pursue Grew's proposal. At the time there was a peace faction in Tokyo trying to open negotiations. Unfortunately, they thought that the Soviet Union would be a proper go-between, not realizing that Stalin was determined to keep the war going until he had entered on schedule in August. If Truman had been willing to include the guarantee about the emperor in the Potsdam Declaration, then perhaps direct talks between the United States and Japan could have brought about surrender without the use of the bomb. But, given the determination of the Japanese military to resist to the bitter end, it still may have taken the atomic shock to force Hirohito to cast his decisive vote for peace. Nevertheless, it is unfortunate that the United States did not at least pursue this promising path to peace. The supreme irony lies in the fact that when Japan finally did surrender, the United States, realizing it needed the emperor's support to end the fighting in Asia and carry out the occupation of Japan, kept Hirohito on as a figurehead ruler.

The real responsibility for the way World War II ended lies with Franklin Roosevelt, not Harry Truman. It was FDR who insisted on the formula of unconditional surrender that robbed Truman of the freedom to offer Japan a token concession, one that would be granted later anyway. Equally important, the insistence that all that was required for a peaceful world was to destroy the evil regimes in Berlin and Tokyo led to the ensuing Cold War as a hostile and suspicious Soviet Union began moving into the resulting vacuum of power in Europe and Asia. The United States felt compelled to contain this outward flow of Soviet power, leading to four decades of confrontation between the two superpowers. It is thus easy for dissenters to argue that World War II was but another example of the twentieth-century American habit of waging perpetual war for perpetual peace.

## The Korean Armistice

Neither unconditional surrender nor peace without victory proved relevant to the Korean War. Forced to return to its original objective—the defense of South Korea—after the Chinese intervened, the Truman administration was ready to settle for a simple end to the fighting. Such an arrangement would give both sides some satisfaction. The Communists could claim they had prevented the United States from conquering all Korea, while the United States could argue that it had invoked collective security successfully to repel North Korea's aggression.

Peace did not come quickly, however. By the end of 1951, armistice negotiations deadlocked over the issue of the forced repatriation of prisoners of war (POWs). Many of the Chinese and North Korean POWs did not want to return to their homelands after the fighting stopped, and President Truman felt it would be morally wrong to force men to live under Communism. Over the objections of U.S. military leaders, whose forces were suffering a thousand casualties a week and who wanted to speed the return of American POWs, Truman insisted that the armistice allow all prisoners the freedom to choose whether or not to be returned. Any other course, he told the American people, "would be repugnant to the fundamental moral and humanitarian principles which underlie our action in Korea."[5]

The Korea stalemate became an issue in the 1952 campaign as the fighting heated up that fall. Although the Republican candidate, Gen. Dwight D. Eisenhower, did not challenge Truman's stand on the POW issue, he did capitalize on the growing public frustration with the war. In late October he made a famous pledge, telling a Detroit audience that, if elected president, "I shall go to Korea."[6] It was a shrewd move. Although he made no commitment and gave no indication of how he would act, the mere promise that the World War II hero would personally visit Korea seemed to suggest that he would find a way to end the bloodbath.

After his victory in November, Eisenhower kept his word. He traveled to Korea in the late fall and found the situation to be grim. He carefully avoided endorsing the military's plans for a new offensive, fearful that such a move would only lead to deeper involvement and increased loss of life. He rejected the advice of his secretary of state, John Foster Dulles, who wanted to give the Chinese "one hell of a licking." Eisenhower later commented that "small attacks on small hills would not end the war."[7]

Another alternative was to threaten the use of nuclear weapons to compel the Communists to negotiate an armistice. Although Dulles and Eisenhower later hinted that it was just such a nuclear threat that broke the stalemate, the evidence is thin.

Certainly the Chinese were aware of the American nuclear capability, and they had at least some reason to fear that Eisenhower and Dulles would be more likely than Truman to employ it. The new president, after authorizing the deployment of atomic weapons to overseas bases, including nearby Okinawa, told his advisers that the Communist leaders "must be scared as hell" by America's nuclear superiority.[8] But Dulles, fearful of touching off a nuclear exchange with the Soviet Union, proved very circumspect in delivering a veiled warning to China by way of India that the United States would be compelled to widen the war if there was no progress toward an armistice soon. Mao and his advisers apparently did not view this as a nuclear threat, fearing instead another Inch'on—an American amphibious attack on the North Korean coastline.

Joseph Stalin's death in early March, 1953, proved to be the catalyst for peace in Korea. Stalin had viewed the stalemate in Korea as being in the Soviet interest; he was willing to accept heavy North Korean and Chinese casualties to keep the Americans tied down in Asia. Within two weeks of his death, however, the new Soviet leadership informed China and North Korea of their interest in a "firm peace" and "the soonest possible conclusion of the war in Korea."[9] Mao and Kim Il Sung, who between them had lost over a million men killed and wounded, ordered their diplomats to negotiate a compromise on the POW issue. As a result, the fighting in Korea ended on July 27, 1953, with the signing of an armistice agreement at Panmunjom.

American leaders could take little satisfaction in the end of the Korean War. The armistice left Korea divided into two mutually antagonistic regimes, each still claiming to be the rightful ruler over the entire peninsula. While the United States could boast of a successful defense of the principle of collective security, it hardly seemed to justify the loss of more than fifty thousand American lives. Truman's reputation would suffer from both his unwise effort to conquer Korea in 1950 and his stubborn insistence on opposing forced repatriation, which prolonged the war and the casualties for nearly two years. The only person who benefitted was President Eisenhower, who fulfilled his implied campaign promise and could claim to have ushered in an era of peace and tranquillity for the rest of the 1950s.

## Better Dead Than Red

Although the Cold War would not end for another thirty-three years, in 1958 the Senate voted to insure that it did not terminate with an American surrender to the Soviet Union. This curious episode began on August 14, 1958, when Sen. Richard Russell, Democratic chairman of the Senate Armed Services Committee, heard an alarming radio report that "shocked [him] beyond expression."[10] The newscaster claimed that the Pentagon had authorized secret studies of the possibility of surrendering to the Soviet Union to avoid destruction in a nuclear showdown.

The source for the radio report was a newspaper article that coupled a Pentagon estimate of American casualties in a nuclear war at between 15 million and 90 million with a RAND Corporation study analyzing the concept of strategic surrender. The air force had subsidized the publication of the RAND study, a book by Paul Kecskemeti examining the World War II experience and arguing that it was often better to negotiate than to insist on unconditional surrender. Unfortunately, he noted in one passage that in the nuclear age, if one side gained a first strike capability over its adversary, "a mere threat of attack might induce the latter to surrender politically."[11]

Despite assurances from President Eisenhower that he would never contemplate surrender, Senator Russell was determined to rule out any possibility of capitulation to the Soviet Union. At a time when the press was predicting a possible missile gap in Russia's favor by the early 1960s, he felt it was vital to reassure the nation. He therefore introduced an amendment to a pending military appropriation bill that would prevent the Pentagon from spending money on any future surrender studies. Russell told the Senate that he hoped God would spare America from "the horrors of a nuclear war." But if the unthinkable happened, he was sure that "the vast majority of our people would prefer to die on their feet . . . than to be making plans for living on their knees as the slaves of the masters of the Kremlin."[12]

Neither Senate majority leader Lyndon Johnson nor his Republican colleagues could persuade Russell not to demand a vote on his "no surrender" amendment. Senator after senator spoke, admitting that while there was little likelihood of such an eventuality they nevertheless supported Russell and would never condone nuclear appeasement. Republican John Sherman Cooper of Kentucky was one of only two senators who had the courage to speak out in opposition (Democrat Richard Neuberger of Oregon was the other). Expressing his faith in the president, Cooper said he was sure that under Eisenhower's leadership America would never surrender. "We will go into the long night," he avowed, "rather than surrender."[13] But his pleas fell on deaf ears. On the evening of August 15, 1958, the Senate voted 88–2 to adopt the Russell amendment. It was now official. The United States would rather face total destruction than live under Communism. At the height of the Cold War, the Senators said they would rather be dead than red.

Fortunately, Americans did not have to make that difficult choice. The feared missile gap never materialized. During the tense Cuban missile crisis the United States had a significant strategic advantage that John F. Kennedy used to force Nikita Khrushchev to withdraw Soviet missiles from Cuba. The end of the Cold War came not with a bang but a whimper as the Soviet economy, weakened by its own structural faults, finally collapsed under the strain of trying to keep up with the United States in the arms race. Yet long before that occurred, the United States had to come to grips with its own imperial overreach in Vietnam.

## Disguised Surrender in Vietnam

Ending American involvement in the Vietnam War took even longer than the earlier escalation. On March 31, 1968, nearly three years after approving the massive buildup of American forces in South Vietnam, LBJ began the peace process by offering to curtail the bombing of North Vietnam and enter into negotiations with Hanoi. For the next five years, the United States clung to its goal of defending an independent South Vietnam before finally agreeing to withdraw its troops.

The long endgame reflected unwillingness on the part of first Lyndon Johnson, and then his successor, Richard Nixon, to admit that the United States had lost the war. Both men continued to insist that the North Vietnamese withdraw their forces and accept the legitimacy of the South Vietnamese government. But Hanoi refused to give up on its plan to unite all of Vietnam under its leadership. The result was a continued deadlock at the negotiating table in Paris while the war continued in Southeast Asia.

Breakthroughs were few and far between. Johnson finally did order a bombing halt in late October, 1968, and talks began in Paris in November. However, the negotiations soon stalled when U.S. negotiators refused to abandon the Saigon government and insisted that the North Vietnamese match any withdrawal of U.S. troops from the south.

Richard Nixon proved to be as adamant as Lyndon Johnson in refusing to become the Old Maid by surrendering South Vietnam to the Communists. He had hinted during the 1968 campaign that he had a plan to end the war honorably, but in reality all he offered was more of the same: a peace that included an independent South Vietnam. Nixon had a chance to end the war quickly and benefit the way Eisenhower had from the Korean armistice, but in 1969 he refused to accept any agreement that did not guarantee the continuation of the Saigon government. With Hanoi equally intent on its goal of a greater Vietnam, the war was destined to continue for four more years.

During that interval, Nixon used a variety of ways to bring American power to bear on a weaker opponent. He relied on a policy of Vietnamization, withdrawing large numbers of U.S. troops while training the South Vietnamese army to take their place. He authorized an invasion of Cambodia in 1970 and an incursion into Laos a year later in a vain effort to halt North Vietnamese infiltration via the Ho Chi Minh Trail. When Hanoi tried to overwhelm South Vietnam's forces with a major offensive in the spring of 1972 Nixon used massive air strikes on North Vietnam's supply lines, as well as the mining of Haiphong harbor, to blunt it. Like Johnson, he believed America's credibility in the world was on the line, and he was determined not to give way. "If we were to lose in Vietnam," he told an associate, "there would have been no respect for the American President . . . because we had the power and didn't use it. . . . We must be credible."[14]

Henry Kissinger, Nixon's national security adviser, tried hard to break the stalemate at the negotiating table. In secret meetings with his North Vietnamese counterpart, Le Duc Tho, Kissinger gave up the demand for mutual withdrawal of forces from South Vietnam, agreeing in 1971 to pull out U.S. troops over a seven-month period in exchange for the return of all American POWs. A possible deal fell through, however, when North Vietnam insisted on the removal of South Vietnam's president, Nguyen Van Thieu. A similar compromise in the fall of 1972, which left the fate of South Vietnam uncertain, failed when Thieu resisted and Nixon refused to pressure him further.

After his reelection in November, 1972, the president decided to step up his efforts to end the war, agreeing to compel South Vietnam to accept a vague settlement in return for his promise of U.S. military support if North Vietnam resorted to force in the future. When Hanoi balked, Nixon began a massive bombing attack on the North Vietnamese capital. At the start of this Christmas bombing campaign, the president told the chairman of the Joint Chiefs of Staff: "I don't want any more of this crap about the fact that we couldn't hit this target or that one. This is your chance to use military power to win this war, and if you don't, I'll consider you responsible."[15] B-52 bombers dropped more than thirty-six thousand tons of bombs on Hanoi over the next twelve days. The bombing finally ended when the North Vietnamese agreed to return to the bargaining table.

The final peace accords accomplished little more than what Nixon might have gotten in 1969. American troops would withdraw in return for the release of all POWs. There was no reciprocal withdrawal of North Vietnamese troops from the south. President Thieu would remain in power, but despite Nixon's promise to help him if North Vietnam resumed hostilities, it was clearly only a question of time before Hanoi achieved its long-sought objective of uniting all of Vietnam under its rule. All Nixon had achieved after four more years of war was a disguised surrender.

The end came two years later. A North Vietnamese offensive quickly led to the collapse of the Saigon government in April, 1975. Nixon himself was gone, forced to resign over Watergate, and his successor, Gerald R. Ford, could not persuade Congress to approve a last-minute effort to save South Vietnam. On April 30, 1975, the last American helicopter left the embassy roof in Saigon, signaling the end of the long and futile American effort in Vietnam.

America's difficulty in bringing the Vietnam War to a quick and merciful end reflects the nation's unwillingness to acknowledge the reality of defeat. Used to winning wars, Americans were not prepared to end one they clearly had lost. Believing that admitting failure would damage America's credibility, the government's stubborn refusal to face facts did much greater harm to the nation's reputation in the world. The United States played its hand to the bitter end in Vietnam. The result was a humiliating withdrawal that brought little honor to those who had fought and died there. If World Wars I and II are examples of the problem America has had translating military victory into lasting peace, then Vietnam revealed that Americans were even less well equipped to handle the consequences of battlefield defeat.

## The Survival of Saddam Hussein

The end of the Gulf War came faster than anyone had expected. Thanks to the intense aerial attacks and meticulous planning, the coalition forces did not suffer the feared high casualties in either the direct attack on Iraqi forces in Kuwait or the sweeping envelopment around their left flank. The rapid progress led to the early liberation of Kuwait, a coalition goal, but failed to draw the Republican Guard into the trap that General Schwarzkopf had set for them with his flanking maneuver. As a result, a significant portion of the Guard and its armor escaped, insuring Saddam Hussein's survival in Baghdad.

The attack across the desert proved to be a brilliant stroke. Led by the VII Corps, American forces swept into western Iraq with little resistance. When Saddam sent three Republican Guard divisions to engage the invaders while the rest of his forces fled north into Iraq, the VII Corps won a major battle, destroying sixty-nine Iraqi tanks and thirty-eight armored personnel carriers. But it was a hollow victory as the Iraqi defeat bought time for the other Republican Guard armored divisions, allowing them to begin crossing the Euphrates. Fear of hitting friendly forces prevented the air force from attacking the fleeing Guard units while the VII Corps regrouped for the final assault on Basra and Highway 8, the only road north.

Meanwhile, a successful air force attack on an Iraqi column fleeing from Kuwait City had important political repercussions. American F-15E fighter-bombers knocked out the lead cars in a thousand-vehicle convoy at Mutla Pass on Highway 6 between Kuwait City and Basra. For the next few hours, American planes strafed the stalled convoy, destroying the cars and trucks, many of them filled with loot from Kuwait, while the Iraqis fled into the countryside. Reporters who viewed the wreckage quickly dubbed it "the highway of death" and talked about the air force conducting a "turkey shoot."[16] Although there were relatively few Iraqi casualties, the incident raised fears in Washington that the United States would be seen as slaughtering an already defeated enemy. President Bush kept telling his advisers that he wanted "a clean end" to the war and expressed his concern that as the Iraqi soldiers "are going out, we're still shooting."[17]

The coalition goal of liberating Kuwait further limited American freedom of action. After Arab troops marched into Kuwait City on the fourth day of the ground war, February 27, 1991, political pressure to bring an end to hostilities began to build in Washington. The United States had achieved its major goal, proving to the world that aggression did not pay, and it seemed to be well on its way toward knocking out a large portion of the Republican Guard. The military, pleased by the low casualty rate, did not want to risk American lives unnecessarily. Bush, intent on eradicating the memory of America's humiliation in Vietnam, had hoped to end the war with the surrender of Saddam Hussein, but he now knew that was impossible.

There was no question of advancing on Baghdad, as some critics later claimed the United States should have done. America's leadership of the coalition ruled that out, as did the fear that such a move, like Truman's decision to cross the 38th Parallel in Korea, would result in a long and costly American involvement in a distant and hostile land. Bush would have preferred that the Iraqi people depose Saddam, but even if they did not, a chastened Iraq would serve as a counterbalance to Iran in the vital Persian Gulf region.

The question, rather, was one of timing. Bush was ready to declare a cease-fire, but he wanted to be sure that the field commander agreed. General Schwarzkopf solved the problem with a dramatic briefing in Riyadh, Saudi Arabia, on February 27. Fearful that the Pentagon would announce the victory, he described the fighting in broad outline, boasting that his forces had decimated the Republican Guard. "The gate is closed," he claimed, "there's no way out."[18] He admitted that escape routes were still open across the Euphrates, but added that any troops who got out would have to leave their tanks and artillery behind.

The field commander was being less than candid. Earlier his subordinates had told him that it would take one more day to close the noose on the Republican Guard. But when General Powell sought his approval for a cease-fire, Schwarzkopf could hardly say no, although he did ask for time to consult with his commanders. They in turn decided not to voice their reservations, being as averse to a confrontation with their superior as Schwarzkopf was in dealing with Washington. The original plan was to halt the fighting at 5 A.M. on February 28. However, as a public relations gesture, Bush moved it forward three hours in order to call it a hundred-hour ground war. When Schwarzkopf subsequently informed his deputy, Lt. Gen. Calvin Waller, of this designation, Waller replied, "That's bullshit."[19]

At nine the evening before, President Bush announced the forthcoming cease-fire to the American people. "Kuwait is liberated," he declared. "Iraq's army is defeated." He went on to avow that the coalition had upheld the principle of collective security in resisting territorial aggression. "This is a victory for the United Nations, for all mankind, and for what is right," he concluded.[20]

In reality, the United States had achieved only half a victory. The liberation of Kuwait fulfilled the coalition's mandate, but the decision to stop the war prematurely allowed a major part of the Republican Guard, along with seven hundred tanks, to escape to Baghdad. Saddam was left with enough military power to crush rebellions by the Shi'ites in the south and the Kurds in the north over the next few months.

President Bush had mixed feelings. He felt he had succeeded in restoring the lost luster of American military power in the aftermath of Vietnam, as well as in liberating Kuwait. But as he wrote in his diary on February 28, 1991: "It hasn't been a clean end—there is no battleship *Missouri* surrender. That is what's missing to make this akin to World War II."[21]

Unlike the famous scene of Japan's leaders bowing to General MacArthur before they signed the surrender documents in Tokyo Bay, the Persian Gulf War ended without Saddam's unconditional surrender. Yet Bush had acted responsibly. He had formed and led a broad international coalition that achieved its stated goal of upholding the Wilsonian principle of collective security. At the same time, he had protected American access to Persian Gulf oil. His only failure stemmed from adding the unrealistic goal of trying to topple Saddam from power. The fact that the president was voted out of office less than two years later while the Iraqi dictator continues to annoy the world with his defiance should not overshadow the fact that the United States achieved a notable victory, as Bush had boasted, "for all mankind."

## Perpetual War for Perpetual Peace

My brief review of the historical record shows that Americans have had great trouble ending wars. All too often, U.S. leaders have failed to realize the close connection between the use of force in wartime and the political process of making peace. Wilson thought that his proclamation of idealistic principles would insure a just and lasting peace; instead he found himself forced to compromise many of his idealistic goals at Versailles, ending up with a treaty that led to a second and even greater world war. The goal of unconditional surrender proved equally misguided. Truman's decision to use the atomic bomb to end the war with Japan has remained a source of controversy, most recently over the *Enola Gay* exhibit at the Smithsonian Institution's National Air and Space Museum in 1996. Guilt over using nuclear weapons to end the war, an act accepted without remorse by those who fought in World War II, has continued to haunt the national conscience. The stalemate in Korea, largely the result of Truman's unwise decision to invade North Korea after Inch'on, has left that nation divided and a trouble spot ever since. In Vietnam, wiser American diplomacy, once U.S. leaders acknowledged that the United States could not prevail by force of arms, could have led to an earlier and less traumatic withdrawal. Finally, Americans continue to live with the consequences of the unhappy ending of the Gulf War. The continued threat posed by Saddam Hussein tends to overshadow the achievement of liberating Kuwait.

What this litany suggests is that, for the United States at least, war is a messy and unpredictable way to deal with international problems. Americans enter into conflicts convinced that they can create a better and more stable world once their enemies are defeated, only to meet with unexpected outcomes and a new set of challenges. Perhaps a more realistic view of war, one that does not raise so many hopes for a brighter future, would be the lesson we should draw from our twentieth-century experience with armed conflict. War is often the only alternative when a nation is confronted with the provocative acts of men like Adolf Hitler and Saddam Hussein, but maybe we should be content with preventing evil from triumphing, rather than seeking to insure that goodness will forever prevail. An appreciation of the continuity between war and peace would serve us well as we prepare to face the problems of the twenty-first century. An understanding of the utopian nature of the Wilsonian quest for enduring peace may be the surest guide for dealing with these future international challenges.

In a sense, Charles Beard and Harry Elmer Barnes were right in labeling America's activist foreign policy since 1898 "perpetual war for perpetual peace." The moral of this epigram for them was that war itself was unwise and unnecessary. They truly believed that the United States could remain aloof from the world, perfecting democracy at home rather than trying to export it to others. But one can also extract a different message: that war, rather than being an exceptional event, is in fact the norm in international affairs. The American mistake was the idealistic belief that peace was the normal human condition and that all the United States had to do to achieve it permanently was to defeat the current threat to its well being. If we can learn to accept the reality that we will have to take up arms periodically to protect and advance the national interest, perhaps then we can learn to limit each conflict to specific and realizable goals. In other words, we can never win the final victory that will usher in an era of lasting peace. All we can hope for, as we engage in perpetual war for perpetual peace, is to contain the violence and strive for at least a brief period of tranquillity before the next armed confrontation.

# Epilogue

The 1990s, the first post–Cold War decade, hardly proved to be the peaceful era that everyone had looked forward to during the years of superpower rivalry. American troops intervened in Somalia and Haiti with mixed results at best, and the entire world ignored the brutal tribal slaughter in Rwanda that killed hundreds of thousands of innocent people.

The breakup of Yugoslavia created the most dangerous threat to world peace. Early in the decade Slovenia and Croatia declared their independence and were able to maintain it after brief but intense fighting with Serbia, led by dictator Slobodan Milosevic. A similar attempt to achieve freedom from Yugoslavia by Bosnia-Herzegovina led to a bitter, three-year civil war fought among Serbs, Muslims and Croats. The Bosnian Serbs, backed and supplied by Milosevic, carried out a policy of "ethnic cleansing," driving Bosnian Muslims out of their homes and farms and laying a deadly siege to the city of Sarajevo. In late 1995, thanks in part to a new Croatian offensive and NATO air strikes, the United States was able to broker a truce at Dayton, Ohio, which left Bosnia divided into three ethnic enclaves. American troops who took part in the international occupation force, originally scheduled to leave within a year, were still enforcing a shaky peace nearly five years later.

The Balkan crisis of the 1990s came to a head in Kosovo in 1999. At the time, ethnic Albanians made up 90 percent of the population in that province, the site of many sacred Serbian monuments and battlefields. Milosevic ordered an end to the province's autonomy in 1989 and imposed Serbian rule. The Kosovars began to resist, with some seeking merely a return to autonomy, and others, who formed the Kosovo Liberation Army (KLA), seeking independence. Serbia responded with brutal repression, beginning a campaign in mid-1998 to destroy the KLA. As fighting intensified and civilian casualties mounted, U.S. diplomat Richard Holbrooke, who had negotiated the Dayton Accords on Bosnia, was able to get Milosevic to agree to a temporary cease-fire in October, 1998. However, renewed Serbian atrocities in early 1999 outraged world opinion and led to a search for a more permanent diplomatic solution at Rambouillet, France, in February. The United States and NATO presented a plan to have a NATO peacekeeping force occupy Kosovo, which would remain under Serbian sovereignty. Both the Serbs and the Albanians refused to sign, but when Secretary of State Madeleine Albright added a provision for a referendum on independence after three years of autonomy, the Albanian delegation agreed to the new terms.

Milosevic, however, refused to give up Kosovo in what amounted to a disguised surrender. Holbrooke and Albright pressed him to sign the agreement, using the threat of NATO bombing that had worked earlier in Bosnia. But the Serbian dictator objected to NATO control of Kosovo, especially to a provision that would allow the peacekeepers to enter Serbia itself in their pacification efforts. The United States and NATO responded on March 24 with a bombing campaign against Serbia designed to achieve a quick solution. But what began as a show of force to bring Milosevic to the bargaining table turned into a much wider conflict. Serbia began a campaign of ruthless ethnic cleansing in Kosovo, driving nearly a million Albanian refugees from the province in the spring of 1999 in complete defiance of the continuing NATO air strikes. The United

States found itself waging another in the series of perpetual wars for perpetual peace.

Three issues stand out in the Kosovo crisis. First, why did the United States decide to use force in the distant Balkans? Was this war by design or by miscalculation? Second, how did the United States fight this conflict? What lay behind the decision to rely on airpower alone to achieve NATO's goals? Finally, how successful was the Clinton administration in achieving its original objectives? Was the resort to force justified in terms of its consequences?

The decision to use force appears to be based on a serious miscalculation of Milosevic as a leader. In earlier confrontations, he had acquiesced in the departure of Slovenia and Croatia from the Yugoslav federation, although not before engaging in heavy fighting. He withdrew his support of the Bosnian Serbs at Dayton, but only after reaching an agreement that allowed them to retain most of the territory they had gained in the civil war there. Moreover, while NATO air strikes had played a role in forcing him to compromise on Bosnia, they were probably not as important a factor as the successful offensive waged by the revitalized Croatian army in northern Bosnia in 1995. In other words, he gave way in the face of superior force but he was still able to claim that he had not abandoned the Serbs in Bosnia.

Kosovo was a different proposition. The historic Serb ties to a province that had become overwhelmingly Albanian made it difficult for him to let it go. His dreams of a greater Serbia had suffered severe shocks, and he was not about to give up such a vital part of Serbia's traditional domain. He also knew that many NATO members were reluctant to follow the aggressive leadership of the United States and Great Britain—Germany, Italy, and Greece were particularly opposed to the use of force. Above all, he counted on NATO's distaste for a bloody ground war in the difficult Balkan terrain to dissuade the United States and its allies from halting his plans to purge Kosovo of its Albanian majority.

President Bill Clinton and Secretary of State Albright believed that a show of force would be enough to persuade the Serbian dictator to accept the Rambouillet plan, which would end the ethnic cleansing and likely lead to an independent Kosovo after three years of NATO peacekeeping. The original bombing strategy reflected the administration's belief in the symbolic use of force. Instead of attacking bridges, power plants, and other parts of the Serbian infrastructure, the NATO attack began with sea- and air-launched cruise missiles that hit a few empty buildings in the dead of night. Concern for avoiding the loss of aircraft, as well as deferring to reluctant NATO allies on the choice of targets, made the initial bombing very ineffective.

When Milosevic, instead of quietly capitulating, responded with his all-out assault on the Kosovars, the United States had no choice but to expand the air campaign, gradually hitting more meaningful targets and inflicting heavy damage on Serbia's infrastructure. What began as a symbolic use of force settled down into a major effort to use airpower to compel a cruel dictator to halt his ethnic cleansing in Kosovo.

The prospect of a longer war forced President Clinton to justify the conflict to the American people. When the bombing began on March 24, he stated American aims in limited terms: "to demonstrate the seriousness of NATO's opposition to aggression," "to deter President Milosevic from continuing and escalating his attacks on helpless civilians," and "if necessary, to damage Serbia's capacity to wage war against Kosovo." Avoiding any specific reference to American national interest, he spoke only of his desire "to leave our children a Europe that is free, peaceful and stable."[1]

As the air war intensified in April, Clinton began to step up the rhetoric. Now NATO was attempting to stamp out "unspeakable brutality" in Kosovo. He spelled out two distinct American goals in the fighting. The first was "to prevent a wider war." In what amounted to a parody of the familiar Cold War domino theory, he spoke of the danger of the war spreading throughout the Balkans and involving Greece, Turkey, Hungary, Poland, and the Czech Republic. "If we were to do nothing," he asserted, "eventually our allies and then the United States would be drawn into a larger conflict, at far-greater risks to our people and far-greater costs."[2]

Even more important, Clinton stressed, was the need to protect innocent people from a brutal dictator. While admitting that the United States could not "respond to every tragedy in every corner of the world," that did not mean "we should do nothing for no one." Portraying Milosevic as a dictator bent on imposing Serbian rule on his neighbors, regardless of their wishes, the president asserted that America's intent was to make him "pay the price of aggression and murder."[3] Clinton, echoing Woodrow Wilson, even went so far as to suggest that the ultimate objective would be to remove Milosevic and install a democratic government in Serbia. Peace in the Balkans, he avowed on April 15, "will require a democratic transition in Serbia, for the region's democracies will never be safe with a belligerent tyranny in their midst."[4]

Thus, what began as a limited use of force to achieve a quick diplomatic solution soon turned into a prolonged campaign against another stubborn dictator. Clinton felt compelled to explain the conflict to the American people in traditional terms. It was an attempt not only to serve the national interest by preventing a wider war in the Balkans but an effort to halt a ruthless aggressor and seek the triumph of the democratic way of life. Suddenly the stability of the Balkans, a region the United States had traditionally avoided, had become a major goal of American foreign policy.

Kosovo marked the first time the United States attempted to fight a war with airpower alone. In Vietnam, air strikes against the north in 1965 were soon followed by the introduction of ground forces in South Vietnam. Although airpower played a much more effective role in the Persian Gulf War, the end came only after the massive ground offensive liberated Kuwait in just one hundred hours. Yet in Kosovo, Clinton stated publicly at the outset that he had no intention of using ground forces.

The guiding principle of the American military effort in the Kosovo conflict was to minimize NATO losses. In part this reflected the post-Vietnam fear that the American people would not accept a large death toll again. But it also stemmed from the need for coalition unity. America's European allies, particularly Germany, were strongly opposed to the use of ground troops in Kosovo, and other NATO members, especially Italy and Greece, backed this position wholeheartedly. While critics complained that President Clinton should at least have retained the option of sending troops into Kosovo, he felt constrained to reassure both the American people and the NATO allies that this was not under consideration.

Yet his decision to rule out a ground war made considerable sense. Kosovo's rugged terrain favored the experienced Serbian army, which would be fighting on its own ground. Supply problems would also have been formidable: the only available ports to unload troops and equipment were in Albania and Greece. Moreover, the downsizing of the U.S. military that took place after the Persian Gulf War had left the United States with a scarcity of well-trained and well-equipped combat forces. Finally, even if Clinton had decided to mount an assault on Kosovo, it would not have stopped the ethnic cleansing already underway. Pentagon planners estimated that such an invasion would require 150,000 troops and could not be carried out before early fall.

When it appeared that Milosevic was willing to ride out the air war, calls for a ground offensive began to increase. In May, British prime minister Tony Blair proposed launching an attack on the Serbian army in Kosovo, but only after it had been sufficiently softened by continued air assaults. Clinton still refused to consider a ground attack, but he did approve plans to send fifty thousand NATO troops to the borders of Kosovo in Albania and Macedonia. Although they were intended as the vanguard for the eventual peacekeeping force in Kosovo, the United States hoped that Milosevic might see such a concentration as evidence of a possible ground attack.

In the end, airpower alone proved successful, in defiance of the conventional wisdom. In a campaign lasting seventy-eight days, NATO pilots flew 37,200 sorties with the loss of only two planes and without the death of a single airman. This achievement was especially remarkable in light of the political restraints imposed by both President Clinton and the NATO alliance. At the outset, Gen. Wesley K. Clark, the NATO commander, ordered his planners to conduct a campaign with the unprecedented restriction that there be "no loss of aircraft."[5] This decision meant heavy reliance on long-distance missile strikes and forced the pilots to stay above fifteen thousand feet to avoid Serbian air defenses.

The NATO allies also limited the nature of the air war. All nineteen members had to approve the targets selected. French president M. Jacques Chirac boasted after the war that he had vetoed any attacks on bridges within the city of Belgrade, as well as many targets in Montenegro that he felt "weren't reasonable or weren't humane." Chirac told the French people that because "We opposed those strikes, they didn't take place."[6]

Despite these restrictions, the NATO air strikes caused serious political repercussions. Several attacks on bridges outside Belgrade led to unexpected civilian casualties when they hit trains and buses crossing them. Errant bombs fell on residential neighborhoods, hospitals, and refugee columns in Kosovo that were mistaken for Serbian armored formations. The most embarrassing incident occurred when, thanks to an out-dated Central Intelligence Agency map, the Chinese embassy in Belgrade was bombed. Three Chinese journalists died, relations with Beijing became very tense, and NATO suspended the bombing of Belgrade for nearly a week.

After the war, the greatest controversy over the air campaign centered on the degree of damage inflicted on the Serbian army. When Milosevic intensified his ethnic cleansing in Kosovo after the air attacks began, NATO found itself helpless to stop the brutal process. The fifteen-thousand-foot restriction made it very difficult to identify and destroy the well-camouflaged and mobile Serbian forces in Kosovo. General Clark lowered the altitude limit to twelve thousand feet and authorized more attacks on Serbian army units in Kosovo, but with questionable results. Although Clark later claimed that NATO planes had destroyed 110 Serb tanks and many more armored personnel carriers, the peacekeepers who entered Kosovo after the cease-fire were surprised at both the high morale of the departing Serbian troops and the number of their tanks and armored vehicles. The Serbs claimed they lost only three tanks and fewer than six hundred men to the NATO air attacks. The use of clever decoys and the ability to remain under cover with no NATO ground forces to flush them out explains why the Serbians were so successful in weathering the air assault. It is hard to challenge the conclusion of Richard Haass of the Brookings Institution, who contends that "air power failed to shape the situation on the ground in Kosovo."[7]

The key to victory, it turned out, was not in Kosovo but in Serbia. The initial attacks on empty barracks and government buildings gradually gave way to a stepped-up campaign against the Serbian infrastructure. The destruction of bridges (except in Belgrade itself), oil refineries, TV stations, and power plants began to cripple the country's economy. When the bombing resumed after the Chinese embassy fiasco, NATO focused on the power grid, ultimately knocking out 60 percent of Serbia's electrical capacity. As the Serbian people began to feel the full pain of the loss of their normal way of life, the political pressure on Milosevic became intense, finally forcing him to return to the bargaining table to spare his nation further damage and ensure his own survival.

Critics claim that the air war failed to save the more than 1 million Kosovars forced to flee their homes after the bombing began. They also contend that NATO did not conduct the air war properly; if the coalition had begun with massive strikes against power plants and the military command-and-control network, Milosevic would have been forced to capitulate much sooner. Yet the fact remains that the air campaign, whatever its flaws, did prove successful. Clinton belied his reputation for indecision and currying public favor; he stuck to his decision to rely on airpower alone and in the end prevailed. Clinton, together with Tony Blair, kept NATO united and stood firm in the face of mounting criticism both at home and abroad. Only a few months after surviving the impeachment challenge in Congress, the president waged a successful war against a brutal dictator, proving once again his ability to rebound. Clinton's victory in Kosovo helped redeem his tarnished presidential reputation. In the future, predicted historian Henry Graff, "I think people will say he fought a war and didn't lose a single man."[8]

The consequences of the Kosovo conflict transcend President Clinton's reputation. In the long run, the war will be judged by the outcome in the Balkans. Did the use of force by the United States do more than stop Milosevic's efforts at ethnic cleansing? Will the United States and its NATO allies be able to fulfill their goal of a multiethnic Kosovo in which the Albanian majority and the Serbian minority live in peace? Or will the world soon be faced with yet more ethnic violence and another round of Balkan wars? Finally, to what extent does Kosovo serve as a model for future American policy? Is the United States now committed to intervention anywhere in the world where there is ethnic turmoil and large-scale human suffering?

The end of the fighting came unexpectedly in early June. The heavy damage to Serbia's infrastructure, along with pressure for a negotiated solution from Russia—Serbia's traditional ally, which was heavily dependent on continued American economic assistance—forced Milosevic to enter into negotiations. Special Russian Balkan envoy Viktor Chernomyrdin and Finnish president Martti Ahtisaari, delivered NATO's terms to Milosevic, who drove a hard bargain. The final agreement called for the withdrawal of Serbian forces from Kosovo and the entry of forty-eight thousand NATO peacekeepers, as well as a Russian contingent, with overall responsibility for the occupation resting with the United Nations. More important from Milosevic's standpoint, Kosovo would remain a multiethnic province under Serbian sovereignty. There would be no Kosovar vote on independence after three years, as called for in the Rambouillet agreement.

Observers quickly divided over the outcome of the Kosovo conflict. Those who supported the NATO action stressed that the coalition, under Clinton's leadership, had stood up to the Serbian dictator and brought an end to the ethnic cleansing. The Kosovars who had been forced to flee could return safely to their homeland under the watchful eye of NATO troops. Most of all, Clinton was proud that he had fought a war for humanitarian reasons. If the United States had not acted, aides reported him saying, "we wouldn't have been able to sleep at night."[9] In a commencement address at the University of Chicago on June 12, 1999, the president expressed his belief that inaction in the face of the human suffering in Kosovo "would have been a terrible mistake. . . . I believe we did a good thing in Kosovo. It is perhaps the first conflict ever fought where no one wanted any land, or money, or geopolitical advantage; we just wanted to stop and reverse ethnic cleansing."[10]

Critics, however, were quick to point out some of the negative consequences of the Kosovo conflict. They argued that the bombing, rather than helping the Kosovars, had hurt them. The withdrawal of two thousand international observers from the beleaguered province allowed Milosevic to expel the Albanians without foreign witnesses to the atrocities his troops committed in the process. "While the unrestrained killings were taking place," wrote one British critic, "tens of thousands of Nato troops were slumped inert over the horizon," and the coalition's planes were "bombing empty office blocks and deserted barracks."[11] Others, like retired Lt. Gen. William Odom of the Hudson Institute, pointed to the survival of Milosevic, the man responsible for the suffering in Kosovo. Odom warned that in the future Milosevic would be "free to destroy the pro-NATO regime in Montenegro, to repress the Hungarian minority in Vojvodina and to cause trouble elsewhere. . . . In other words, the present peace deal could only be a truce that allows all sides to prepare for the next and larger war."[12]

The most serious limitation of the Kosovo peace agreement related to the sovereignty of the province itself. Unlike Rambouillet, there was no provision for a plebiscite for future independence; Kosovo was to remain an integral part of Serbia. As Council on Foreign Relations fellow Michael Mandelbaum observed ironically, NATO "intervened in a civil war and defeated one side, but embraced the position of the party it had defeated on the issue over which the war had been fought."[13]

Whatever the legal issues, it seems almost certain that Kosovo will not remain Serbian for long. In spite of the Clinton administration's goal of a multiethnic democracy in the province, the Albanian majority, led by the KLA, appears determined to carry out ethnic cleansing in reverse. Less than three months after the fighting stopped, 180,000 Serbs, out of a prewar population of two hundred thousand, had fled Kosovo in fear of Albanian retribution. Despite the efforts of NATO peacekeepers to protect the remaining Serbs, it is unlikely many will stay unless they are granted a separate enclave in eastern Kosovo in direct violation of stated American policy. The most likely outcome is an independent Kosovo made up entirely of ethnic Albanians—a result which, while acceptable on moral grounds, would violate the whole rationale for the NATO intervention in the first place.

The most difficult aspect of the Kosovo conflict is its significance as a precedent. President Clinton has hailed it as the first truly humanitarian American war, a claim with considerable merit. The Spanish-American War used the plight of Cubans to justify a conflict that ended up with American territorial gains. In World War I, Wilson's crusade for democracy would not have been possible without German submarine attacks on American shipping and concern over the European balance of power. World War II witnessed a clear joining of moral outrage over the brutal aggression of the Axis powers with a genuine fear for national security, made evident by the Japanese attack on Pearl Harbor. In Korea and Vietnam, the Cold War–inspired fear of Communism outweighed considerations of what was best for those America was fighting to defend in those Asian lands. And in the Persian Gulf War, genuine outrage over the brutal Iraqi invasion of Kuwait might not have led to U.S. intervention had Saddam not threatened America's vital Persian Gulf oil lifeline.

Yet the concept of fighting humanitarian wars raises some troubling issues. In the future, how will the United States decide when ethnic tensions within a sovereign nation are severe enough to justify American action? Given the Clinton administration's refusal to act in Rwanda in 1994, will we only intervene to protect human rights in Europe? The image of the United States as the world's policeman, deciding when and whether to intervene in the internal affairs of other nations is hardly reassuring. How does America avoid the charge of imperialism when it invokes the same justification European powers used in the nineteenth century to extend their control over large parts of Africa and Asia?

The implications of a Clinton "doctrine" calling for the United States to base its foreign policy on defending human rights around the world is frightening. However justified the nation may have been to intervene in Kosovo on humanitarian grounds, it set a dangerous precedent for the next century. The failure to rescue the Kosovars before they were forced to flee their homeland and the continued uncertainty over the province's future, with the possibility of future American involvement in Balkan wars, makes this a dubious model for tomorrow's policy makers.

The adventure in Kosovo is yet another example of American involvement in perpetual wars for perpetual peace. It may have been necessary to ease the American conscience, but it should not be held out as an example to be followed in the future. Wars do not lead to peace; instead they give rise to new tensions and dilemmas that result in new conflicts. The only reality, observed journalist Michael Elliott, is that "whatever adjective you stick in front of it, war is terrible. . . . Some wars are necessary; some wars are just. But no war is good."[14]

# Notes

## Introduction

1. Harry Elmer Barnes, ed., *Perpetual War for Perpetual Peace.*
2. Ibid., pp. viii, 68; Justus D. Doenecke, *Not to the Swift: The Old Isolationists in the Cold War Era,* p. 100.

## Chapter One. Entering Wars

1. George Frost Kennan, *American Diplomacy, 1900–1950,* p. 66.
2. James D. Richardson, ed., *Messages and Public Papers of the Presidents,* p. 4:442.
3. Robert A. Divine, et al., *America Past and Present,* p. 443.
4. Howard Jones, *The Course of American Diplomacy,* p. 255.
5. Arthur S. Link, ed., *The Papers of Woodrow Wilson,* p. 46:525.
6. Ibid., pp. 46:526–27.
7. George Creel, *The War, the World and Wilson,* pp. 98–99.
8. U.S. Department of State, *Peace and War: United States Foreign Policy, 1931–1941,* pp. 271–72.
9. Thomas A. Bailey, *A Diplomatic History of the American People,* p. 722.
10. State Department, *Peace and War,* p. 741.
11. James MacGregor Burns, *Roosevelt: The Soldier of Freedom,* p. 165.
12. Charles C. Tansill, *Back Door to War: The Roosevelt Foreign Policy, 1933–1941.*
13. Harry S. Truman, *Memoirs,* p. 2:333.

14. Walter LaFeber, *America, Russia, and the Cold War, 1945–1992*, p. 105.
15. Mike Gravel, ed., *The Pentagon Papers*, pp. 1:37–38.
16. Daniel Ellsberg, *Papers on the War*, pp. 102–106.
17. *New York Times, The Pentagon Papers*, p. 492.
18. Edward E. Moise, *Tonkin Gulf and the Escalation of the Vietnam War*, p. 253.
19. George C. Herring, *America's Longest War: The United States and Vietnam, 1950–1975*, p. 144.
20. Ibid., p. 189.
21. Jean Edward Smith, *George Bush's War*, pp. 55–56.
22. Lawrence Freedman and Efraim Karsh, *The Gulf Conflict, 1990–1991: Diplomacy and War in the New World Order*, pp. 90, 93–94.
23. Roger Hilsman, *George Bush vs. Saddam Hussein*, p. 47.
24. Freedman and Karsh, *Gulf Conflict*, p. 215.
25. James A. Baker III, *The Politics of Diplomacy: Revolution, War and Peace, 1989–1992*, p. 336; Hilsman, *Bush vs. Saddam*, p. 336.
26. Freedman and Karsh, *Gulf Conflict*, p. 219.

## Chapter Two. Fighting Wars

1. Kennan, *American Diplomacy*, p. 84.
2. Daniel M. Smith, *The Great Departure: The United States and World War I, 1914–1920*, p. 86, emphasis in original text.
3. Link, *Papers of Wilson*, p. 46:538.
4. Gaddis Smith, *American Diplomacy during the Second World War, 1941–1945*, p. 46.
5. Burns, *Roosevelt*, p. 323.
6. Kent Roberts Greenfield, *American Strategy in World War II: A Reconsideration*, p. 19.
7. Chester Wilmot, *The Struggle for Europe*, p. 693.
8. Burton I. Kaufman, *The Korean War: Challenges in Crisis, Credibility, and Command*, p. 56.

9. Ibid., p. 56.

10. Robert J. Donovan, *Tumultuous Years: The Presidency of Harry S Truman, 1949–1953*, p. 276.

11. D. Clayton James, *The Years of MacArthur: Triumph and Disaster, 1945–1964*, p. 590.

12. Kaufman, *Korean War*, p. 107.

13. James, *MacArthur*, p. 616.

14. Michael R. Beschloss, ed., *Taking Charge: The Johnson White House Tapes, 1963–1964*, p. 369.

15. George C. Herring, *LBJ and Vietnam: A Different Kind of War*, pp. 20–21.

16. Herring, *America's Longest War*, p. 166.

17. Larry Berman, *Lyndon Johnson's War: The Road to Stalemate in Vietnam*, p. 117.

18. Eric F. Goldman, *The Tragedy of Lyndon Johnson*, p. 491.

19. Herring, *LBJ and Vietnam*, p. 140.

20. William C. Westmoreland, *A Soldier Reports*, p. 445.

21. Harry G. Summers, Jr., *On Strategy: A Critical Analysis of the Vietnam War*, p. 105.

22. Colin L. Powell, *My American Journey*, pp. 509–10.

23. Freedman and Karsh, *Gulf Conflict*, p. 309.

24. William M. Arkin and Rick Atkinson, "Fog of War," *Washington Post*, Aug. 1, 1998.

25. Michael R. Gordon and Gen. Bernard E. Trainor, *The Generals' War: The Inside Story of the Conflict in the Gulf*, p. 374.

26. Ibid., p. xii.

## Chapter Three. Ending Wars

1. Bailey, *Diplomatic History*, p. 263.

2. Link, *Papers of Wilson*, p. 63:503.

3. Thomas A. Bailey, *Woodrow Wilson and the Great Betrayal*, p. 277.

4. Paul Kecskemeti, *Strategic Surrender: The Politics of Victory and Defeat*, p. 164.

5. Kaufman, *Korean War,* p. 240.

6. Ibid., p. 292.

7. Emmet John Hughes, *The Ordeal of Power: A Political Memoir of the Eisenhower Years,* p. 105; Dwight D. Eisenhower, *Mandate for Change, 1953–1956,* p. 95.

8. John Lewis Gaddis, *We Now Know: Rethinking Cold War History,* p. 110.

9. Ibid., p. 109.

10. Gilbert C. Fite, *Richard B. Russell: Senator from Georgia,* p. 365.

11. Kecskemeti, *Strategic Surrender,* p. 247.

12. *Congressional Record,* Aug. 14, 1958, p. 17517.

13. Ibid., p. 17609.

14. Herring, *America's Longest War,* p. 273.

15. Ibid., p. 280.

16. Freedman and Karsh, *Gulf Conflict,* p. 402.

17. George Bush and Brent Scowcroft, *A World Transformed,* pp. 482, 484.

18. Freedman and Karsh, *Gulf Conflict,* p. 404.

19. Gordon and Trainor, *Generals' War,* p. 423.

20. Bush and Scowcroft, *World Transformed,* p. 486.

21. Ibid., p. 487.

## Epilogue

1. Transcript of speech by Clinton, *New York Times* Internet Web Site (www.nytimes.com), Mar. 24, 1999.

2. Ibid., Apr. 2, 1999.

3. Ibid.

4. Ibid., Apr. 16, 1999.

5. William Drozdiak and Dana Priest, "NATO's Cautious Air Strategy Comes Under Fire," *Washington Post* Internet Web Site (www.washingtonpost.com), May 16, 1999.

6. Internet web site of the French Embassy in the United Kingdom (www.ambafrance.org.uk), July 14, 1999.

7. As quoted in Richard J. Newman, "Did Air Power Alone Really Carry the Day?" *U.S. News & World Report* Internet Web Site (www.usnews.com), June 14, 1999. The KLA demonstrated the importance of ground forces in assisting the air war. A KLA offensive in the last week of the war enabled American B-52s and A-10 attack planes to inflict heavy casualties on the Serbian forces opposing them in western Kosovo. See Peter Grier and James N. Thurman, "Lessons of a Remote-control War," *Christian Science Monitor* Internet Web Site (www.csmonitor.com), June 11, 1999.

8. Terence Hunt, "Clinton's Fortunes Suddenly Rising," Associated Press Internet Web Site (www.wire.ap.org), June 4, 1999.

9. Michael Elliott, "The Lessons of a 'War of Values,'" *Newsweek* Internet Web Site (www.newsweek.com), June 28, 1999.

10. Cable News Network (CNN) Internet Web Site (www.cnn.com), July 12, 1999.

11. Simon Jenkins, "On Your Way, Morality," *Times* (London) Web Site (www.sunday-times.com), June 23, 1999.

12. William E. Odom, "A Conditional Surrender," *New York Times* Internet Web Site, June 6, 1999.

13. Thomas L. Friedman, "Kosovo's Three Wars," *New York Times* Internet Web Site, Aug. 6, 1999.

14. Elliott, "Lessons."

# Bibliography

Bailey, Thomas A. *A Diplomatic History of the American People.* 10th ed. Englewood Cliffs, N.J.: Prentice-Hall, 1980.

————. *Woodrow Wilson and the Great Betrayal.* Chicago: Quadrangle, 1963.

Baker, James A., III. *The Politics of Diplomacy: Revolution, War and Peace, 1989–1992.* New York: G. P. Putnam's Sons, 1995.

Barnes, Harry Elmer, ed. *Perpetual War for Perpetual Peace.* Caldwell, Idaho: Caxton, 1953.

Berman, Larry. *Lyndon Johnson's War: The Road to Stalemate in Vietnam.* New York: Norton, 1989.

Beschloss, Michael R., ed. *Taking Charge: The Johnson White House Tapes, 1963–1964.* New York: Simon and Schuster, 1997.

Burns, James MacGregor. *Roosevelt: The Soldier of Freedom.* New York: Harcourt Brace Jovanovich, 1970.

Bush, George, and Brent Scowcroft. *A World Transformed.* New York: Knopf, 1998.

Creel, George. *The War, the World and Wilson.* New York: Harper and Brothers, 1920.

Divine, Robert A., et al. *America Past and Present.* 4th ed. New York: HarperCollins, 1995.

Doenecke, Justus D. *Not to the Swift: The Old Isolationists in the Cold War Era.* Lewisburg, Pa.: Bucknell University Press, 1979.

Donovan, Robert J. *Tumultuous Years: The Presidency of Harry S Truman, 1949–1953.* New York: Norton, 1982.

Eisenhower, Dwight D. *Mandate for Change, 1953–1956.* Garden City, N.Y.: Doubleday, 1963.

Ellsberg, Daniel. *Papers on the War.* New York: Simon and Schuster, 1972.

Fite, Gilbert C. *Richard B. Russell: Senator from Georgia.* Chapel Hill: University of North Carolina Press, 1991.

Freedman, Lawrence, and Efraim Karsh. *The Gulf Conflict, 1990–1991: Diplomacy and War in the New World Order.* Princeton, N.J.: Princeton University Press, 1993.

Gaddis, John Lewis. *We Now Know: Rethinking Cold War History.* New York: Oxford University Press, 1997.

Goldman, Eric F. *The Tragedy of Lyndon Johnson.* New York: Dell, 1974.

Gordon, Michael R., and Gen. Bernard E. Trainor. *The Generals' War: The Inside Story of the Conflict in the Gulf.* Boston: Little, Brown, 1995.

Greenfield, Kent Roberts. *American Strategy in World War II: A Reconsideration.* Baltimore: Johns Hopkins University Press, 1963.

Herring, George C. *America's Longest War: The United States and Vietnam, 1950–1975.* 3d ed. New York: McGraw-Hill, 1996.

———. *LBJ and Vietnam: A Different Kind of War.* Austin: University of Texas Press, 1994.

Hilsman, Roger. *George Bush vs. Saddam Hussein.* Novato, Calif.: Lyford, 1992.

Hughes, Emmet John. *The Ordeal of Power: A Political Memoir of the Eisenhower Years.* New York: Atheneum, 1975.

James, D. Clayton. *The Years of MacArthur: Triumph and Disaster, 1945–1964.* Boston: Houghton Mifflin, 1985.

Jones, Howard. *The Course of American Diplomacy.* 2d ed. Chicago: Dorsey, 1988.

Kaufman, Burton I. *The Korean War: Challenges in Crisis, Credibility, and Command.* 2d ed. New York: McGraw-Hill, 1997.

Kecskemeti, Paul. *Strategic Surrender: The Politics of Victory and Defeat.* Stanford, Calif.: Stanford University Press, 1958.

Kennan, George Frost. *American Diplomacy, 1900–1950.* Chicago: University of Chicago Press, 1951.

LaFeber, Walter. *America, Russia, and the Cold War, 1945–1992.* 7th ed. New York: McGraw-Hill, 1993.

Link, Arthur S., ed. *The Papers of Woodrow Wilson.* 69 vols. Princeton, N.J.: Princeton University Press, 1966–94.

Moise, Edward E. *Tonkin Gulf and the Escalation of the Vietnam War.* Chapel Hill: University of North Carolina Press, 1996.

New York Times. *The Pentagon Papers.* New York: Bantam, 1971.

Powell, Colin L. *My American Journey.* New York: Random House, 1995.

Richardson, James D., ed. *Messages and Public Papers of the Presidents.* 10 vols. Washington, D.C.: Government Printing Office, 1896–99.

Gravel, Mike, ed. *The Pentagon Papers.* 5 vols. Boston: Beacon, 1971.

Smith, Daniel M. *The Great Departure: The United States and World War I, 1914–1920.* New York: John Wiley, 1965.

Smith, Gaddis. *American Diplomacy during the Second World War, 1941–1945.* 2d ed. New York: Random House, 1985.

Smith, Jean Edward. *George Bush's War.* New York: Henry Holt, 1992.

Summers, Harry G., Jr. *On Strategy: A Critical Analysis of the Vietnam War.* New York: Dell, 1984.

Tansill, Charles C. *Back Door to War: The Roosevelt Foreign Policy, 1933–1941.* Chicago: Henry Regnery, 1952.

Truman, Harry S. *Memoirs.* 2 vols. Garden City, N.Y.: Doubleday, 1955–56.

U.S. Department of State. *Peace and War: United States Foreign Policy, 1931–1941.* Washington, D.C.: Government Printing Office, 1943.

Westmoreland, William C. *A Soldier Reports.* New York: Dell, 1980.

Wilmot, Chester. *The Struggle for Europe.* New York: Harper and Brothers, 1952.

# Index

bombing (*cont.*)
Japan, 71–73; halted in Vietnam, 78; Christmas (1972) raids on Hanoi, 79–80; of Serbia in Kosovo conflict, 85–96; of Chinese embassy in Belgrade, 93, 94; and end of Kosovo conflict, 96
Borah, William, 37
Bosnia, 37; civil war in, 87–88
Bosnian Muslims, 87
Bosnian Serbs, 87,89
Bradley, Omar N.: on unconditional surrender, 46–47; and Korean War, 50
Brookings Institution, 94
Bundy, McGeorge, 32, 52
Burma, 70
Bush, George: and origins of Gulf War, 33–36; and conduct of Gulf War, 55–59; and end of Gulf War, 82–84
Byrnes, James, 71–72

California, 40, 41, 64
Cambodia, 79
Canada, 64
Casablanca conference, 44
casualties: estimates of for invasion of Japan, 71; in Gulf War, 71; in Kosovo conflict, 93–94
Central Intelligence Agency, 93
Central Powers, 19, 41. *See also* Austro-Hungarian Empire; Germany

Chernomyrdin, Viktor, 95
China: Japan invades, 25; and split with Soviet Union, 30; communists gain control over, 47; intervenes in Korean War, 48–50; and U.S. conduct of Vietnam War, 51–52, 55; and end of World War II, 69–70; and end of Korean War, 73–75; embassy in Belgrade bombed, 93, 94
Chirac, M. Jacques, 93
Churchill, Winston: critical of unconditional surrender, 44; and conduct of World War II, 45–47; and end of World War II, 70
Civil War, 13, 18, 40, 65
Clark, Wesley K., 93, 94
Clausewitz, Carl von, 46
Clemenceau, Georges, 66
Clinton, Bill: and origins of Kosovo conflict, 89–91; and air war against Serbia, 91–95; and consequences of Kosovo conflict, 95–98
Clinton "doctrine," 98
Cold War, 90, 98; end of, 14, 15; and Korean War, 47; relationship to Gulf War, 57; origins of, 60, 73; and "no surrender" amendment, 76–77
collective security: in Korean War, 28; and origins of Gulf

War, 34, 35–36, 37; advocated by Woodrow Wilson, 42; and conduct of Gulf War, 56, 60; and Senate rejection of League of Nations, 67–69; and end of Korean War, 75; upheld in Gulf War, 83–84

Committee on Public Information, 42

Confederacy, 18, 40

Congress: declares war on Mexico, 18; declares war on Germany in 1917, 21; repeals arms embargo, 23; passes Lend-Lease Act, 24; declares war against Japan, 26; and Korean War, 27; passes Tonkin Gulf resolution, 31; and end of Mexican War, 64; opposes further aid to South Vietnam, 80

containment, 47

Cooper, John Sherman, 77

Council on Foreign Relations, 97

credibility: and Vietnam War, 30; and end of Vietnam war, 80

credibility gap, 32

Croatia, 87, 89

cross-channel invasion. *See* second front

Cuba, 97; and origins of Spanish-American War, 18–19; gains limited independence, 40, 41; becomes U.S. protectorate, 65; and missile crisis, 77

Cuban missile crisis, 77

Czechoslovakia, 23

Czech Republic, 90

Dayton peace accords, 87–88, 89

D-Day. *See* second front

Democratic party, 52

Desert Shield. *See* Operation Desert Shield

Desert Storm. *See* Operation Desert Storm

destroyers-for-bases deal, 24–25

Dewey, George, 65

Dien Bien Phu, 29

domino theory, 55; and Kosovo conflict, 90

Dulles, John Foster, 74–75

Dutch East Indies, 26. *See also* Indonesia

Egypt: and origins of Gulf War, 34, 36; and conduct of Gulf War, 59

Eisenhower, Dwight D., 37; and Vietnam, 29, 30; opposes thrust to Berlin, 46; accepts German surrender, 70; and end of Korean War, 74–76, 78; and "no surrender" amendment, 76–77

election of 1952, 74

election of 1964, 31
election of 1968, 78
election of 1972, 79
Elliott, Michael, 99
Emancipation Proclamation, 40
enclave strategy, 55
England. *See* Great Britain
*Enola Gay,* 84
*Ethiopia,* 68
ethnic cleansing: Kosovars by Serbs, 90, 93–96; in reverse, 97
Euphrates river, 59, 81, 82
exceptionalism. *See* American exceptionalism
Exocet missile, 33

Fahd, King, 34
Ford, Gerald R., 80
Fort Sumter, 18
Four Policemen, 69
Fourteen Points, 42, 43; and Paris peace conference, 66
France, 13; in World War I, 19–21; in World War II, 23; and Vietnam, 29; opposes Wilson's war aims, 41–42; liberated in 1944, 46; and Kosovo conflict, 93
freedom of the seas. *See* neutral rights
French and Indian War, 13
French Indochina: Japan invades, 26. *See also* North Vietnam; South Vietnam

George, David Lloyd, 66
Germany, 32, 97; in World War I, 19–20; U.S. enters World War I against, 21–22; and U.S. entry into World War II, 22–27; and unconditional surrender, 43–47; defeated in World War I, 43, 60; defeated in World War II, 60; and Paris peace conference, 66–67; and Kosovo conflict, 89, 92
Glaspie, April, 33
Goldwater, Barry, 31
Gordon, Michael, 58, 59
Grant, Ulysses, 44, 65
Great Britain: and American Revolution, 13; in World War I, 19–21; and American entry into World War II, 23–24; opposes Wilson's war aims, 41–42; and ending of War of 1812, 63–64; and end of World War II, 69–70; and Kosovo conflict, 89, 92
Greater East Asia Co-Prosperity Sphere, 25
"Great Scud Hunt," 57–58
Great Society, 51
Great War. *See* World War I
Greece, 89, 90, 92
Greenland, 25
Grew, Joseph, 71–72
Gulf of Tonkin incident. *See* Tonkin Gulf incident

Polk, James K.: and origins of Mexican War, 17–18; and conduct of Mexican War, 40; and end of Mexican War, 64

Potsdam Declaration, 72

Powell, Colin L.: and conduct of Gulf War, 56–57, 59; and end of Gulf War, 83

prisoners of war (POWs): and Korean armistice negotiations, 74–75; and end of Vietnam War, 79–80

Puerto Rico, 40

quagmire analogy, 29

Queen of Spades. See "Old Maid" analogy

Rambouillet plan, 88, 90, 97

RAND Corporation, 76

reparations, 66–67

Republican Guard: and conduct of Gulf War, 57–59; escapes, 81–83

Republican party, 47–50, 74

Republic of Korea. See South Korea

Republic of Vietnam. See South Vietnam

revisionist historians: on twentieth-century American wars, 14; on Vietnam War, 54

Rhineland, 66

Ridgway, Matthew B., 49

Rio Grande, 17, 18, 64

Roosevelt, Franklin D., 28, 32; and entry into World War II, 14, 22–27; advocates unconditional surrender policy, 43–47; and conduct of World War II, 60; and end of World War II, 69–70, 73

Roosevelt, Theodore, 65

Russell, Richard B.: and Vietnam War, 52; sponsors "no surrender" amendment, 76–77

Russia: in World War I, 19; and Wilson's war aims, 41; and Napoleonic Wars, 53; role in ending Kosovo conflict, 95. See also Soviet Union

Rwanda, 87, 98

Saddam Hussein: orders invasion of Kuwait, 33–34; Bush compares to Hitler, 34–36; and conduct of Gulf War, 56–59, 60; and end of Gulf War, 81–84, 85; threatens U.S. oil lifeline, 98

San Francisco conference, 69

Saudi Arabia: and origins of Gulf War, 33–34; and conduct of Gulf War, 56–59; and end of Gulf War, 82

Schwarzkopf, H. Norman: and conduct of Gulf War, 56–58; and end of Gulf War, 81–83